PRICE ACTION
TRADING

PRICE ACTION
TRADING

**A Step-By-Step Guide to Learn Technical Analysis,
Trading Strategies & Candlestick Patterns**

INDRAZITH SHANTHARAJ

MANJUL

Manjul Publishing House

First published in India by

Manjul Publishing House
• C-16, Sector 3, Noida, Uttar Pradesh 201301 – India
Website: www.manjulindia.com

Registered Office:
• 10, Nishat Colony, Bhopal 462 003 – India

Distribution Centres
Ahmedabad, Bengaluru, Bhopal, Kolkata, Chennai,
Hyderabad, Mumbai, New Delhi, Pune

First edition published in 2021,
This edition first published by Manjul Publishing House in 2023
All rights reserved

ISBN 978-93-5543-451-7

Printed and bound in India by Nutech Print Services

Disclaimer

This book is sold with the understanding that the author is not engaged in rendering legal, accounting, or any kind of advice while publishing this book. Each individual's risk appetite and expectation from the market are different. All ideas, opinions expressed or implied herein, information, charts, or examples contained in the lessons are for informational and educational purposes only and should not be constructed as a recommendation to invest and trade in the market. The author disclaims any liability, loss, or risk resulting, directly or indirectly, from the use or application of any contents of the book.

Technical analysis is a study of past performance, and past performance does not guarantee future performance. Investors and traders are advised to take the services of a competent expert before making any investment or trading decision.

Disclaimer

Dedicated to my mentor,
Keshav Kumar. B
*who gave me the strength to bounce
back in life.*

Contents

Preface

After writing three books on the stock market, I thought I would never write another on the same topic. However, after completing a 25-day pan-India road trip with two of my close buddies, I started thinking: how could I skip writing a book on price action? A sense of urgency and uneasiness began to push me to write about price action trading.

I visited the same guesthouse I mentioned in my book *How To Make Money With Breakout Trading* and stayed there for a few days. During those days, things became clearer in my mind, and I completed this book.

This book explains how to take successful trades using raw price action and provides a detailed explanation on price and volume, along with guidelines to take up trading as a full-time career.

Let's begin!

Acknowledgments

I would like to thank the many people who helped me in putting this book together — my 'trading gurus', who taught me everything I know about trading.

I would like to thank *TradingView* for providing all the charts used in this book.

Also the who for their immense help in spreading awareness about my books. They are Sanket Gajjar (@ sanstocktrader), Harneet Singh (@traderharneet), Rachit Jain (@rachitpjain), and Rajarshita (@rajarshitas). More power to you guys!

Thanks to Tony, who helped with editing and proofreading.

I have a big list of friends who have supported me in all my book ventures. I will be forever grateful to all of them.

Indrazith Shantharaj
April 2021

1

Why I Ditched Technical Indicators

Let me clarify one thing in the beginning. This book is not about glorifying price action trading and condemning indicators. It is all about sharing in-depth information on price action trading, a unique approach to seeing price-volume relationships, and also how to switch to full-time trading.

I have a crazy friend who does ultra-crazy things in his life and career. He was my engineering classmate, and I have known him for 20 years. He used to disappear during college days and working holidays and would appear all of a sudden one day before the exams. He used to beg close friends to share some of their notes on the subjects just before the exam, but still managed to secure a top-5 position every semester.

My friend ditched all the campus placement offers and instead opted to travel throughout India by train. For the next 3 months, he travelled to the different cities of India. When he came back from his trip, most of us had already started working at I.T. companies. Instead of following the traditional route, he started his career with a BPO call center job.

After 2 years of night shifts at his call center job, he wanted to switch his career to I.T. All of us discouraged him, saying it was too late for him to get into an I.T. job. But he was able to get a development role in a small I.T. firm. He was initially rejected during the interview, but he asked the panel of interviewers two questions:

1) "I didn't have any call center experience, but I was still able to get the *Employee of the Year* award at my current company. So, how can you be so sure that I won't perform here (in I.T.)?"

2) "How can you reject my candidacy without testing my abilities? Please give me an opportunity for 3 months. Don't pay me any salary. If I perform well during the 3 months, give me the offer; otherwise, you can throw me out."

Again, he was able to get the role. He worked there for 3 years, and when he was ready to move on, the company offered a percentage of its stake to retain him. He rejected the offer and moved on. He is still in touch with me, but doesn't disclose anything about his profession. He has been in the US for many years, and there is a strong rumor among our friends that he is working on a secret project for the US government (as he previously worked on the Aadhaar project in India).

I would need to write a separate book to explain all his

qualities. But to keep it short, he took adventurous and crazy decisions throughout his life and emerged as a winner in all of them, except one.

That one exception is the stock market, and that incident pushed me to consider trading on a serious note. Until then, I was not very serious about markets. I used to buy and sell some shares, but never thought of trading as a career.

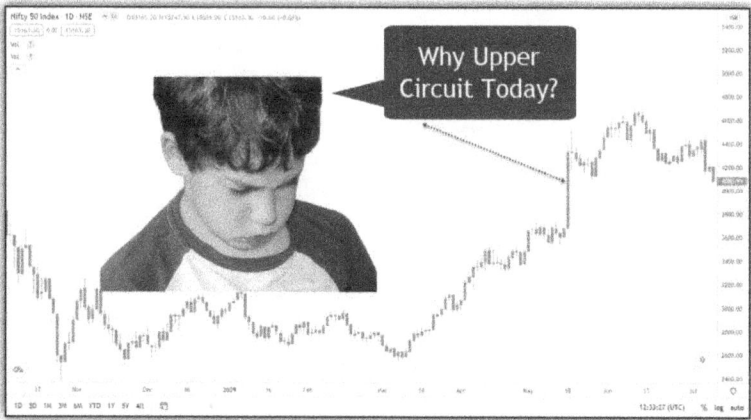

It was 18 May 2009, and it was a Monday.

Nifty had hit the **upper circuit** on that day.

It was a significant and shocking experience for all traders.

All the traders expected a big fall because they thought none of the groups would get the majority in the Union elections. But the election results were announced on Saturday, and the UPA group had acquired the majority.

People started expecting a further fall because many thought that the UPA group was not favorable for markets (that was not my view, just what I heard from many people in those days).

My friend also had a similar view, and hence he had bought a lot of short positions in Nifty using margin (in those days, margin rules were not strict).

But to everyone's surprise, Nifty showed a positive open on 18 May 2009, and within a few minutes, it had hit the upper circuit. I couldn't believe this move and failed to even calculate how much money my friend had lost. I tried calling him, but there was no response from him. After a week, he appeared and shared how much money he had lost. It was a significant amount (at least for the people who had started their career just 3-4 years ago).

Until then, I was a happy soul. I did my fair share of work at the office, loved my intense sessions at the gym, and enjoyed my trips every weekend. But this incident haunted me and raised a big question in my heart. For the first time, I became serious, and simultaneously very curious, about the markets!

Coming back to indicators, I don't hate them and I'm not against them. I do enjoy studying their behavior in different market conditions. Indicators help beginners as they bring some discipline into their trading (otherwise, they will take a lot of trades in 1-2 days only to lose all their money). Besides, it also helps algo traders to develop some rules in their trading systems. But I don't use any of them in my trading as they are not necessary for me.

I have seen a few successful traders who use only price action trading. I have seen some profitable traders who use

1-2 indicators in their trading system.

But I have seen many traders who lose money with naked price action trading as well as with indicators. Hence, debating price action trading vs. indicators is a waste of time. I suggest picking the one which suits your personality. This book gives a detailed overview of price action trading and can give you an edge if you choose this route.

Listed below are the reasons why I ditched technical indicators.

Indicators Don't Dictate the Price

I feel sad for some people when they come with queries like, *"RSI is at 30 for XYZ stock, which is an oversold zone. Can I buy XYZ now?"*, or *"ABCD stock is at 200 DMA, hence it cannot fall from here. Can I accumulate some position?"*

Their question itself indicates the ambiguity. They are specifying the sure-shot movement of the price (due to RSI or DMA levels), but they are also looking for suggestions on whether to buy, which is strange, isn't it?

The price doesn't know or care whether the RSI is in an oversold zone or that it's close to 200 DMA. It efficiently does what it has to do. If the price falls further, the RSI level will also fall further, but at a slower rate, and the moving average will start moving down slowly.

So it is better to remember that, as the name suggests, 'indicators' give indications and don't dictate the price. Any fluctuations in the price will also bring changes to the indicators.

Let's take a few examples to understand this concept.

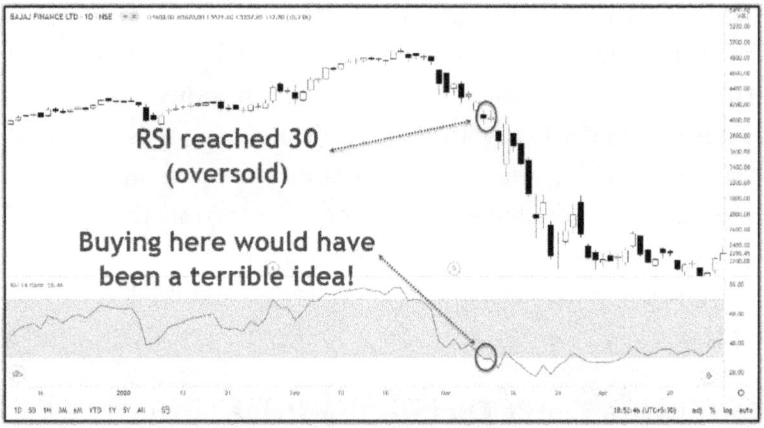

Image 1.1 – *Failure of RSI – overbought (Bajaj Finance)*

If you look at Image 1.1, buying straight away when the RSI reached 30 levels (which is an oversold zone) would have been a terrible idea, and this trade would have ended with a significant loss. As I said earlier, the price doesn't know or care about RSI movements.

Image 1.2 – *Failure of 200 DMA – support concept (USD-CAD)*

Price Action Trading

If you look at Image 1.2, buying straight away when the price reached 200 DMA would have been a bad idea, and again this trade would have ended with a significant loss. I can go on with many more indicators, but I don't want to make this a boring book. I want to simply and effectively convey some essential concepts. The key takeaway is: indicators don't dictate the price! Never take a trade just because an indicator shows a certain level.

Indicators Ignore Human Psychology

"What has happened in the past will happen again.
This is because Markets are driven by humans, and
human nature never changes."
– Jesse Livermore

"Whenever I have had the patience to wait for the
market to arrive at what I call a Pivotal Point
before I started to trade; I have always made money
in my operations."
– Jesse Livermore

These are two quotes by the world-famous trader Jesse Livermore. If you read carefully, you will see that they indicate the importance of human psychology. Hence, this psychology will be reflected at certain key levels in price. One can name them pivotal points, support and resistance zones, supply and demand zones, etc.

Millions of people trade in a stock/index, and their combined actions result in the up or down movement of the price. Hence, there will be a few pivotal points in any stock or index, and planning a trade near them will always provide trades with good risk-reward ratios.

75 is a key level here

Image 1.3 – *Key level concept (BEL)*

If you look at Image 1.3, 75 price level acted as a critical level. Whenever the sellers pushed the price to break this level, a strong buyer accumulated and prevented the fall. Hence, there is a higher probability that the same level will also play a crucial role in the future (unless the big buyer at 75 changes his view).

But all the indicators fail to identify these crucial price levels. It doesn't matter whether you are using RSI, Bollinger Bands, stochastics, or some crazy combination of your own indicators. They fail to identify these crucial levels, and hence you miss many such good trade opportunities.

Do you agree?

Indicators Are Delayed by Nature

You can pick any indicator, but none of them generate trading signals along with the price. There will always be some delay compared to the price (this is common sense, as most of the indicators are derived from the price).

I will provide one simple example to explain the same.

Most of you know that EMA crossover is a primary and popular trading system in the trading community.

A simple system is a combination of 10 EMA and 50 EMA. A buy signal is generated when the 10 EMA crosses 50 EMA from the downside, and a sell signal is generated when the same 10 EMA crosses 50 EMA from the upside.

Image 1.4 – *Entry based on MA crossover*

If you look at Image 1.4, 10 EMA crossed 50 EMA from the downside on 20 May. Hence, an entry will come at 121.53 on 22 May (above the high of the crossover candle). It is a late entry compared to price action trading.

Image 1.5 – *Entry based on price action*

If you look at Image 1.5, there was a decisive break out of the resistance trend line on 19 May, and the entry would have been on 20 May at 120.7 level. We would have been in the trade 2 days earlier compared to the MA crossover trading system.

At this stage, one might argue that if we reduce the duration of the MA (for example, from 10 EMA to 5 EMA) in the MA crossover system, it might generate the entry at an earlier stage.

I do agree with that.

But I have a question – is it a good idea to keep on adjusting this for every stock/index you trade? Or is it better to focus on the price, which is simple, yet powerful and gives fantastic trading results?

Indicators Overcomplicate Trading

How many indicators are there in the market?

1,000? 5,000? Maybe 10,000?

There is no end to this number, as anyone can develop an indicator using any online platform such as *TradingView*, *Chartink*, or *GoCharting*.

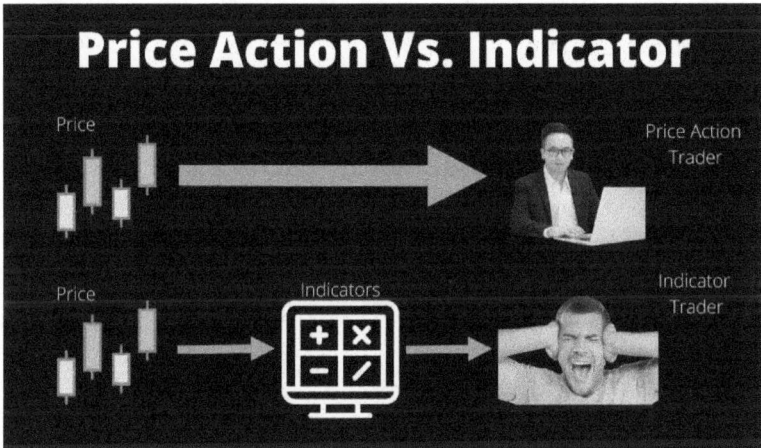

The next question is which indicator to choose among the big list of these indicators.

Even if a trader chooses 2-3 indicators, they can come up with different readings at any time. Isn't that so?

Now, don't get me wrong. I don't want to denounce indicators. My concern is that most people add 4-5 indicators to the chart, wait for some crossovers or overbought/oversold scenarios, and then pull the trigger. In the end, they don't even know what instrument they are buying or selling.

After some time, these traders feel bad when they don't see good results, and then what do they do?

They start looking for one more indicator to add to their trading system, thinking it will fix the problem. It's a vicious cycle!

From a logical perspective, I don't see much difference between a price action trader and an indicator-based trader because both are trying to analyze the price; they're just using different approaches.

Let me explain.

A price action trader studies the price directly.

Most of the indicators are derived from the price. Hence, an indicator trader is also studying the price, but indirectly.

Don't you think it's better to study the price directly instead of investigating the same price using different indicators?

I will leave the choice to you!

2

A Quick Intro to Price Action Trading

What Is Price Action?

'Price action' means price fluctuations of a stock or index in the given market.

On any trading day, from open to close, the price keeps on changing. This variation is nothing but price action.

Image 2.1 – *A simple example of price action trading (Bank Nifty)*

Image 2.1 shows a Bank Nifty 5-minute chart from 24 Dec 2020, where the price varied from 30,007 (low) to 30,546 (high). This variation is nothing but price action.

What Is Price Action Trading?

Price action trading is a trading concept in which a trader reads the chart and makes subjective trading decisions based on the price movements, rather than relying on technical indicators or any other factors.

In simple words, traders use only *price* and *volume* to make any trading decision.

Image 2.2 – *An example of price action trading (Nifty)*

In Image 2.2, you can see that only a price chart is used to make trading decisions. Traders can also use volume information along with the price chart to plan a trade. This is nothing but price action trading.

The three essential components of trading are (in this

order):

1. Price—it advertises all the opportunities.
2. Time—it regulates all the opportunities.
3. Volume—it measures the success or failure of all the advertised opportunities.

Volume is essential, as 80% of the trading volume is given by 20% of the big players.

Hence, price and volume information are more than enough to succeed with positional trading, BTST trading, and long-term trading.

One has to master the 'time' parameter if one is interested in short-term trading, such as intraday trading or scalping. I have covered this topic in detail in Chapter 5.

How Do You Use Price Action Trading?

Traders need to spend some time getting a fair idea about price action trading, as unlike other indicators, it will not generate any buy or sell signals.

Price Action Trading

Identification of key price levels

PRICE ACTION TRADING

Entry at support

Exit at resistance

It consists of 3 steps:

1) Identification of key levels
2) Entry at support
3) Exit at resistance

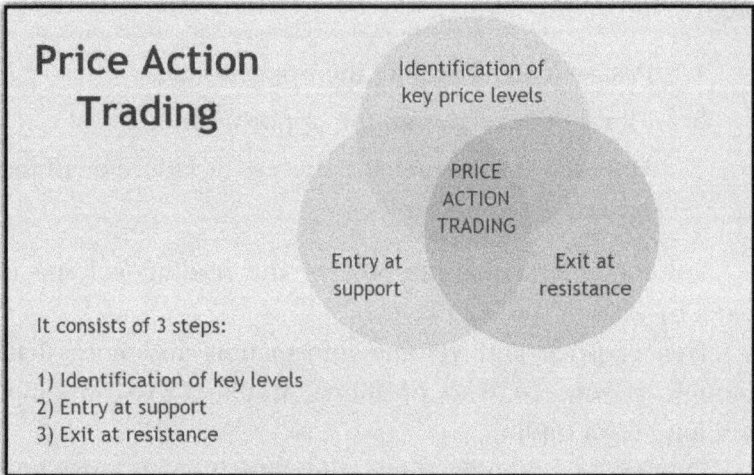

It involves three steps:

1. Identifying key price levels using any method like drawing trend lines, pivot points, supply-demand zones, round numbers, etc.

2. Planning an entry based on the candlestick patterns at key price levels (for beginners) or using raw price action concepts (for experts).

3. Similar to Step 2, planning an exit based on the candlestick patterns or raw price action at key price levels.

When 'Left' Became 'Right' for a Shooter!

Károly Takács was born in Budapest and served in the Hungarian army. From his childhood days, he was interested in only one sport: shooting. His main ambition in life was to win an Olympic gold medal in the sport for his country.

By 1936, he was already a world-class shooter, but he didn't get a chance to participate in the 1936 Summer Olympics as he was a sergeant, and only commissioned officers were allowed to compete in the Olympics.

Takács didn't lose hope, and he kept on practicing his favorite sport. Fortunately for him, after the 1936 Summer Olympics, this restriction on non-officers was removed by the Hungarian army, and hence he was free to participate in the 1940 Tokyo Olympics.

So, he started practicing even harder this time around. He used to spend many hours every day practicing his shooting. But life had other plans for him. In 1938, during a military drill, a grenade exploded in his hand and he lost half of his forearm.

Can you imagine the situation he was in? All his dreams were shattered. He was in the hospital for over a month. When he came back home, he didn't give up practicing. He started everything from the beginning, but this time using his left hand!

Apart from eating and sleeping, he spent most of his time practicing. After a few months of training with his left hand, he turned up for the Hungarian National Championships in 1939.

All the other shooters assumed he had come to watch the competition and offered him their sympathy. But he said, "*I am not here for your sympathetic words. I am here to compete with all of you!*" He secured first place in the competition, to everyone's surprise, and he was automatically eligible for the next Olympics.

Once again, life had other plans for him. Due to the outbreak of the Second World War, both the 1940 and 1944 Olympics were canceled. He was aged 34 in 1944. For most Olympic athletes, the 30s means retirement (even today!). Surprisingly, Takács didn't give up his training, and once again, he was eligible for the 1948 London Olympics. He was already 38 at the time.

During those years, Carlos Enrique Díaz Sáenz Valiente was the world record holder, and he asked Takács why he was in London. Takács's answer to that question was simple and clear: *"I am here to learn!"*

What happened next should be written in golden print in the history books. Not only did Takács win the gold medal, he also bested the world record by 10 points!

Takács then appeared in the 1952 Helsinki Olympics and won the gold medal once again at the age of 42! Valiente (his competitor and the previous world record holder) showered compliments on him and said, *"You have learned more than enough; now it's time to teach me!"*

Now, for all traders who have lost money in trading, there are 2 takeaways from this story:

1. There is no such thing as failure in life. There are only difficult situations that test our character. So, if you have lost money trading, then accept it. If you don't accept it, your mind will not be open to learning. Loss is part of the game, and we are not supposed to repeat the same mistakes in this business.

2. You have lost money because you failed to stick with one trading concept. A basic understanding of 10 different trading concepts will not fetch you money in trading. But a deep understanding of one trading system, along with proper risk management, can yield success in trading.

Always remember these two quotes:

"All you need is one pattern to make a living!"
– Linda Raschke

"I fear not the man who has practiced 10,000 kicks once, but I fear the man who has practiced one kick 10,000 times."
– Bruce Lee

3

Never Underestimate Support and Resistance

As explained earlier, two things play a crucial role in price action trading:

1. Identification of key price levels.

2. Confirmation from the price (either through candlestick patterns or through price acceptance/ rejection).

The 'key price levels' can be identified through many methods, but identifying them through support/resistance by drawing trend lines is the most effective method.

Many traders consider support and resistance concepts as basic trading concepts, and thus they look for some complicated analysis.

But simple things can create wonders in life as well as in trading. I request you to have an open mind and read this chapter thoroughly. I promise you that your ideas and understanding of support and resistance will change forever.

A trader who uses an indicator will have a reference level with an indicator to plan a trade. It can be simple concepts like MA crossover, Bollinger Band breakout, or overbought/oversold scenario. However, a price action trader doesn't have this luxury, as he has only price and volume in his arsenal.

One can only use volume for **confirmation** in the trade setup. Hence, a price action trader has to depend entirely on the price to plan his trades.

It appears as a drawback to the price action traders. But in my opinion, it is a boon for them because they have to study the price in-depth, which is where support and resistance play a crucial role.

How To Draw Trend Lines

A trend line is a straight line drawn on a chart by connecting two or more price peaks, which reveals the script's trend, support and resistance points, and allows one to spot any excellent trade opportunities.

Here are some useful references for drawing a trend line:

1. Try to connect a larger number of peaks (a minimum of 2 peaks is mandatory).

2. The slope of the trend line should be less than 45 degrees (this is the sign of a healthy trend).

3. The price should respect the trend line.

Image 3.1 – *Example of a valid trend line (TCS)*

Image 3.1 shows an example of a valid trend line. It has connected around 8 price peaks. The slope of the trend line (w.r.t. the imaginary horizontal line) is less than 45 degrees, and the price has respected the trend line from the beginning to the end.

Image 3.2 – *Example of an invalid trend line (USD-JPY)*

The trend line which is drawn in Image 3.2 is invalid because it has not respected the trend line.

The power of a trend line decreases when the price doesn't respect it in between. Always look to draw a clear trend line connecting many price peaks.

Image 3.3 – *Example of an invalid trend line (USD-INR)*

Once again, the trend line which is drawn in Image 3.3 is invalid. Because the slope of the trend line is more than 45 degrees (compared to the imaginary horizontal line), it is not a sign of a healthy trend. So, it's better to ignore such a trend line.

What Is Support?

A support is the price level at which demand is strong enough to prevent any further fall in the price.

Image 3.4 – *Example of a support trend line (Tesla, Inc.)*

Image 3.4 shows an example of a support trend line.

The logic is straightforward. People remember their entry or exit levels either because of pleasure or pain. It feels pleasurable to make profits and painful to lose money.

Hence, whenever the price falls towards the support and gets cheaper, buyers become more inclined to accumulate the stock. By the time the price reaches the support level, it is evident that the demand will overcome the supply and prevent the price from falling below the support.

In Image 3.4, whenever the price corrected to 58-59 levels, buyers accumulated the stock, and hence it bounced from this level.

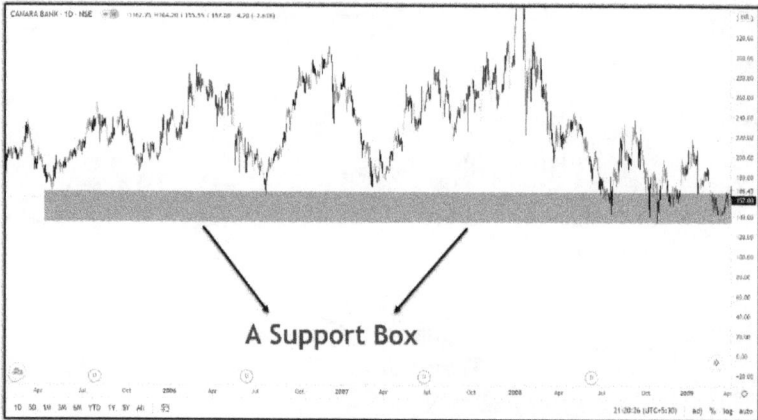

Image 3.5 – *Example of a support box (Canara Bank)*

The market is dynamic, and we can't expect that a single price level acts as the support every time. Sometimes, a small range of price levels will serve as support, which can be called a support box.

In Image 3.5, the price range between 130-160 acted as a support box.

What Is Resistance?

A resistance is a price level at which selling is strong enough to prevent the price from rising further.

Image 3.6 – *Example of a resistance trend line (Intel Corp)*

Image 3.6 shows an example of a resistance trend line. The price level 53 acted as resistance.

As the price moves towards resistance, sellers will be more active, and buyers will be less inclined to buy. By the time the price reaches the resistance level, the supply will overcome the demand and stop the price from rising above the resistance.

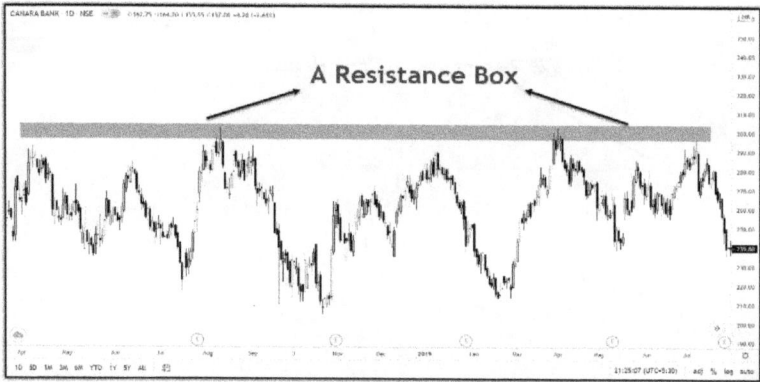

Image 3.7 – *Example of a resistance box (Canara Bank)*

Like a support box, a range of price levels often acts as resistance, which can be recognized as a resistance box.

In Image 3.7, the price range between 290-300 served as the resistance.

Variations of Support and Resistance

There is no rule in the market saying that support and resistance lines have to be perfectly horizontal lines. These support and resistance trend lines often come with a small angle, which is also acceptable.

Image 3.8 – *Example of an angled resistance trend line (NVIDIA Corp)*

Image 3.8 shows an example of an angled resistance trend line. Whenever the price bounced towards the angled resistance trend line, sellers entered, and their force pushed the price to the downside.

Image 3.9 – *Example of an angled support trend line (IMPINJ INC)*

Image 3.9 shows an example of an angled support trend line.

Whenever the price corrected towards the angled support trend line, buyers entered and started buying, and their force pushed the price to the upside.

I am not in a position to give a valid explanation of why and how these angled trend lines work.

However, I have seen it works very well with the market. Hence, I have deployed them in my trading.

Fatal Mistakes Every Trader Should Avoid

Do you know why many traders don't get good results with support and resistance trading concepts? Can you think of any reason why many traders don't believe in or use support and resistance trading concepts in their trading?

It all points to one simple reason.

They assume that a support trend line always prevents the fall and a resistance trend line always resists the bounce.

Besides, they fail to understand *when* the price will take support at the support line or break the support line. The same explanation goes for the resistance line.

Can you think of any better reason? I am sure there is no other reason.

What if you develop the ability to understand whether the price will take support at a support trend line or not, and whether the price will take resistance at a resistance trend line or not?

Then you could make profitable trades most of the time, right?

Chapters 4 and 5 explain this concept in detail. But it would be best if you lost the primary assumption about the infallibility of these lines. A support level may not act as support every time, and a resistance level may not act as resistance every single time.

Then why use support and resistance?

I am sure the above question has popped up in your mind now. But the answer is simple.

When the price fails to take support at the support trend line, it gives a big move in the opposite direction, and if we can take this trade, it increases our profits!

Image 3.10 – *A break of the support line resulted in a big move downside (LT)*

Image 3.10 shows an example of the failure of the support line. There is a good support trend line on the chart, but when the price reached the support trend line on 25th and 26th of Feb, it failed to take support due to the absence of buyers. Hence, it resulted in a big move to the downside.

What if you could foresee this and opted for a short trade after the breakdown of the support trend line instead of waiting to take a long trade? You would have made damn good profits, right? This is the reason we need support and resistance trend lines for price action trading.

Image 3.11 – *A break of the resistance line resulted in a big move upside (CEAT LTD)*

Image 3.11 shows an example of a failure of the resistance line. There is a good resistance trend line on the chart, but when the price breached the resistance trend line on the 14th of March, it resulted in a big move to the upside.

Again, what if you knew early on that the price would not take resistance that time? One could take a better entry in the right direction, correct?

Welcome to the exciting world of PRICE ACTION TRADING!

The real essence of price action trading starts in the next chapter. But I request you to read and understand this chapter thoroughly as this is the core foundation for it.

4

10 Candlestick Patterns To Step-Up Your Trading

I will repeat once again. Two things are crucial in price action trading to identify profitable trade opportunities: 1) Identification of key price levels, and 2) Confirmation or rejection of the price.

In the last chapter, we covered different aspects of identifying key price levels using trend lines. This chapter focuses on 10 powerful candlestick patterns used for confirmation/rejection of the price at key price levels.

Please note that we are not supposed to use these patterns independently. We need to check for these patterns only at the key price levels.

There are thousands of candlestick patterns present in the world of technical analysis. Do you think studying and memorizing all of them is practically possible?

Heck, no!

Then what is a better way to shortlist them?

It's better to shortlist the candlestick patterns based on

two parameters:

1. **Impact of the pattern**
2. **Repeated occurrence of the pattern**

Because if a candlestick pattern has less impact, then it is not useful. Similarly, if a candlestick pattern is powerful but rarely occurs, then again, it is of no use.

Keeping these two parameters in mind, here are some powerful patterns that occur very frequently across all timeframes.

Bullish Engulfing

Engulfing candles tend to signal a reversal of the current trend/swing in the market. It involves two candles, with the latter candle 'engulfing' the previous candle's entire body.

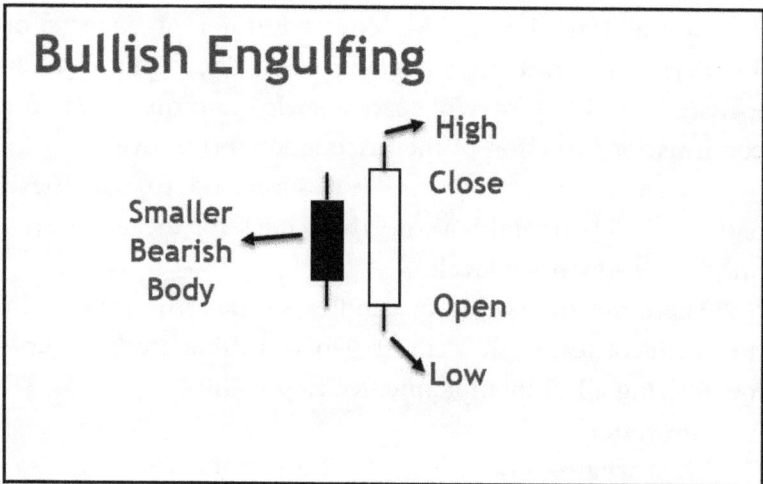

Image 4.1 – *Bullish engulfing pattern*

In the bullish engulfing pattern, the first candle is a small bearish candle. The second candle opens below the first bearish candle and trades lower than the bearish candle, but due to the entry of powerful bulls, it witnesses a close above the bearish candle. Hence, it engulfs the first bearish candle.

It is bullish in nature.

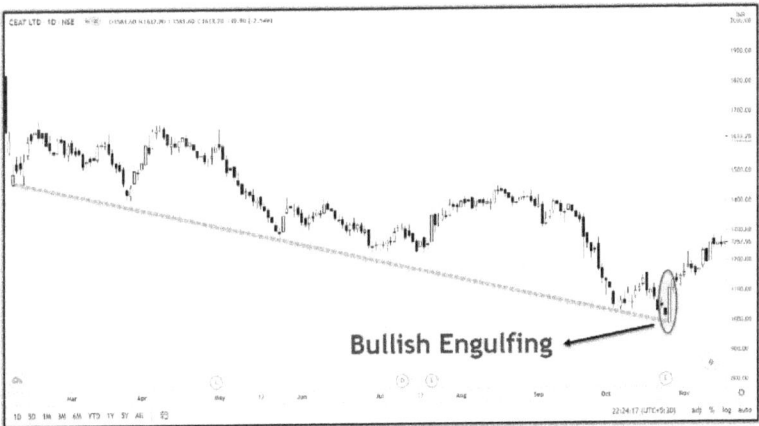

Image 4.2 – *Example of a bullish engulfing pattern (CEAT LTD)*

Image 4.3 – *Example of a bullish engulfing pattern (Jacobs Engineering)*

Images 4.2 and 4.3 are examples of bullish engulfing. The price is in a downtrend/swing, and the bullish engulfing pattern appeared at the support trend line. The price rallied on the upside after displaying the bullish engulfing pattern.

Bearish Engulfing

Engulfing candles tend to signal a reversal of the current trend/swing in the market. It involves two candles, with the latter candle 'engulfing' the previous candle's entire body.

Bearish Engulfing

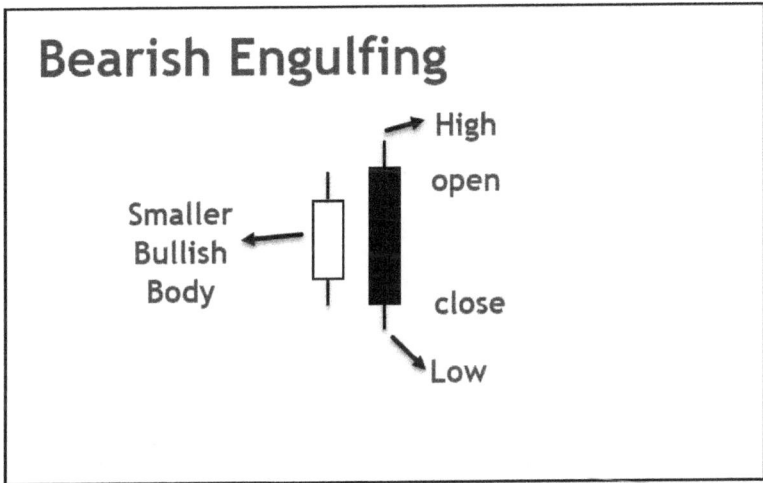

Image 4.4 – *Bearish engulfing pattern*

In the bearish engulfing pattern, the first candle is a small bullish candle.

The second candle opens above the first bullish candle and trades higher than the bullish candle. Still, due to the entry of powerful sellers, it witnesses a close below the bullish candle. Hence, it engulfs the first bullish candle.

It is bearish in nature.

Image 4.5 – *Example of a bearish engulfing pattern (SBIN)*

Image 4.6 – *Example of a bearish engulfing pattern (Bank Nifty)*

Images 4.5 and 4.6 are examples of bearish engulfing. The price was in an uptrend/swing, and the bearish engulfing pattern appeared at the resistance trend line. The price fell after forming the bearish engulfing pattern.

Hammer Pattern

When a stock price trades significantly lower than the open price, it bounces back due to the sudden entry of bulls. It closes a little below or above the open price, which results in the hammer pattern.

If it occurs at a critical support level, then there is a high probability of a reversal in the price chart.

Image 4.7 – *Example of a hammer pattern (Bajaj Finance)*

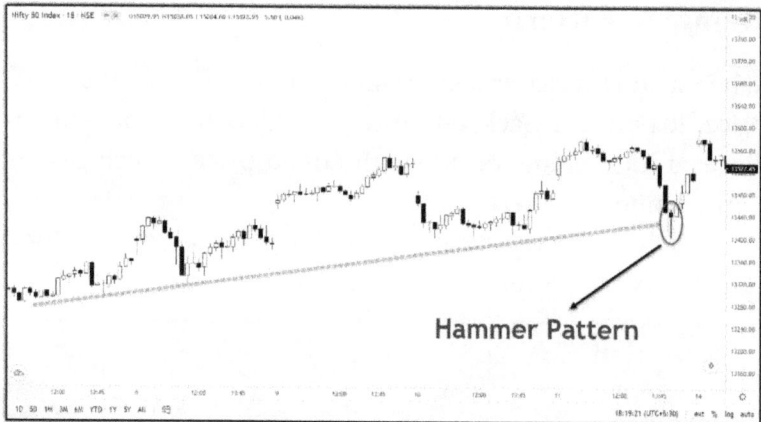

Image 4.8 – *Example of a hammer pattern (Nifty)*

Images 4.7 and 4.8 are examples of a hammer pattern. It is called that since the shape looks like a hammer. In this pattern, the lower shadow is at least twice the size of the real body.

Hanging Man Pattern

This looks similar to a hammer pattern. However, it occurs at the end of the uptrend and resembles a hanging man from the top, hence the name. It indicates the potential reversal of the price from the uptrend.

If it occurs at a critical resistance level, then there is a high probability of a reversal in the price.

Image 4.9 – *Example of a hanging man pattern (KELLOGG)*

Image 4.10 – *Example of a hanging man pattern (TATA Power)*

Images 4.9 and 4.10 display hanging man patterns. In Image 4.9, the price was in an uptrend, and the price displayed the hanging man precisely at the resistance line. In Image 4.10, the trend was down, but the hanging man appeared at the upswing within the downtrend.

This indicates that the buyers have lost their strength to push the price to the upside. Hence, there is a higher probability of the price reversing from that level.

Harami Pattern

Just like engulfing, there are two kinds of Harami patterns:

1. Bullish Harami
2. Bearish Harami

The word 'Harami' means 'pregnant lady' in Japanese. This pattern resembles a pregnant lady, and hence got its name.

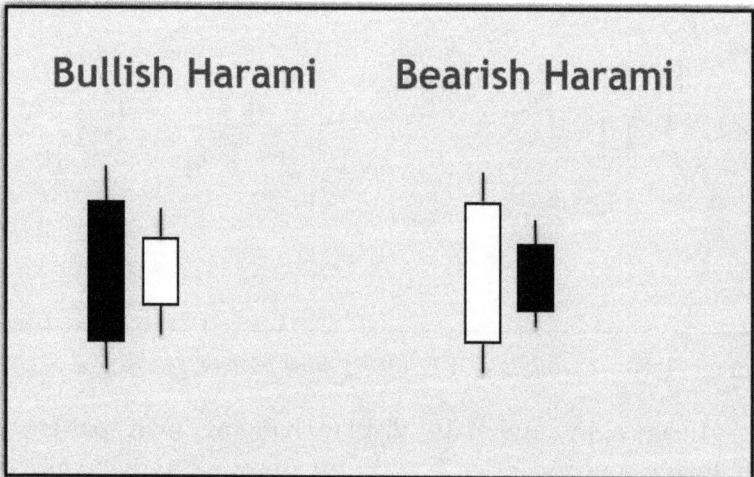

Image 4.11 – *Bullish Harami and bearish Harami patterns*

Bullish Harami includes a big bearish candle first, followed by a small bullish candle in the middle. It indicates that the selling is over, and that there is a high probability of the price going upward.

Bearish Harami includes a big bullish candle first, followed by a small bearish candle in the middle. It indicates that the buying is over, and that there is a high probability of the price going in the downside direction.

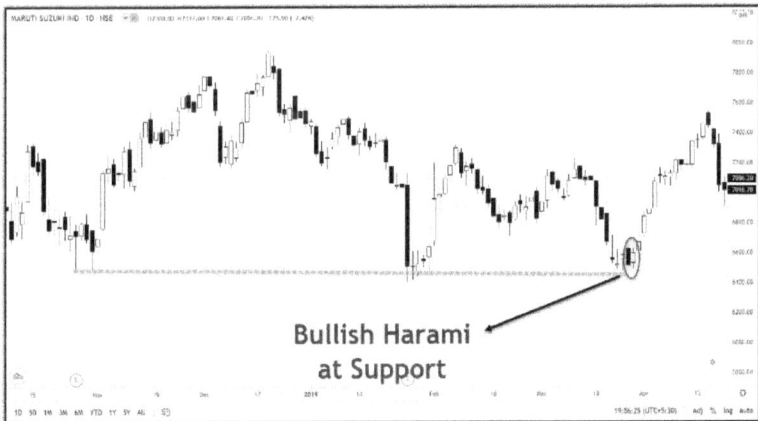

Image 4.12 – *Example of a bullish Harami pattern (Maruti)*

Images 4.12 and 4.13 show examples of bullish Harami and bearish Harami patterns respectively.

Image 4.13 – *Example of a bearish Harami pattern (DLF)*

Morning Star Pattern

A morning star pattern consists of three candlesticks which occur in a downtrend and often indicate the beginning of an uptrend.

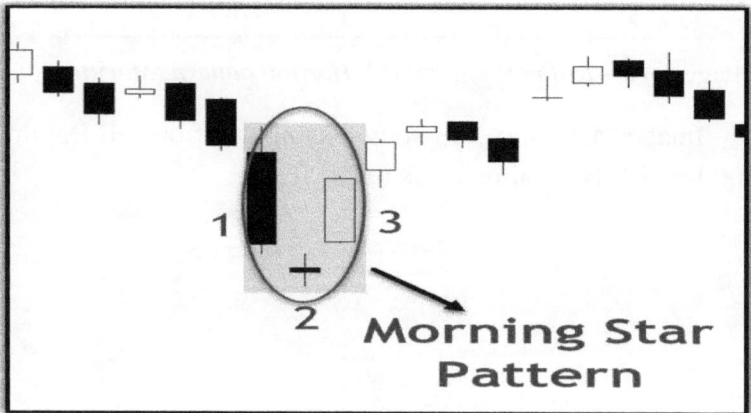

Image 4.14 – *Morning star pattern*

Image 4.15 – *Example of a morning star pattern (TATA Steel)*

It consists of a 1-2-3 formation in a downtrend, indicating the sign of a change in the trend. The first candle is bearish, the second candle indicates indecision, and the third candle indicates the bullish behavior of the price.

Evening Star Pattern

It is similar to the morning star pattern, but goes in the opposite direction. This pattern consists of three candlesticks that occur in an uptrend and indicate the beginning of a downtrend.

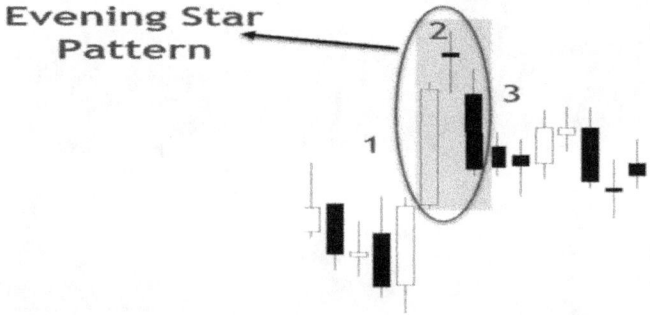

Image 4.16 – *Evening star pattern*

Image 4.17 – *Example of an evening star pattern (GBP-USD)*

Similar to morning star patterns, this pattern also consists of a 1-2-3 formation, but in the opposite direction. It indicates a downtrend. The first candle is bullish, the second candle indicates indecision, and the third candle indicates the bearish behavior of the price.

Doji Pattern

In a doji pattern, the open and close prices will be nearly equal for the selected time period. It is a neutral pattern that indicates indecision.

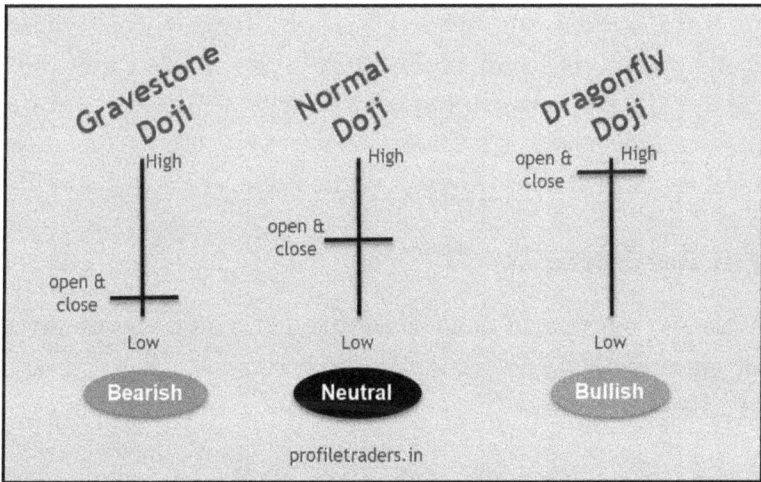

Image 4.18 – *Doji pattern variations*

Image 4.18 shows the different variations of doji. In all three types, the price closed at the open level. However, based on the location of the open/close, it is possible to identify the sentiment behind it.

In a **gravestone doji**, the open and price level will be at the bottom. It indicates that buyers attempted to push the price upside in this period, but they lacked the power to drive the price upside. Hence, it closed at the same open level. We can expect only a downside move until the price negates this pattern.

In a **dragonfly doji**, the situation is precisely the opposite. In this case, sellers tried to push the price downside, but they failed, and hence the price closed at the top. Therefore, we can expect only an upside move until the price negates this pattern.

In a normal doji (also called **long-legged doji**), there is not much clarity in the price. Besides, it also indicates the equal fight between buyers and sellers. Hence, it shows perfect indecision. It's always better to wait for the next candle completion if we get a normal doji.

Pin Bar Patterns

A pin bar consists of one candlestick bar, and it represents a strong reversal and rejection of the price.

Usually, pin bars have a smaller body and a long tail.

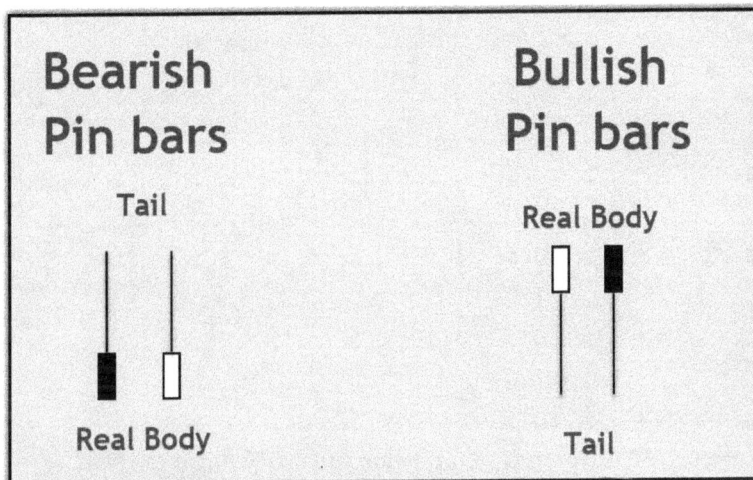

Image 4.19 – *Pin bar patterns*

Again, this pattern has two types: 1) Bullish pin bars and 2) Bearish pin bars.

Bullish pin bars are similar to the hammer pattern. In both types of pin bars, the color of the body doesn't matter much. A longer tail is crucial as it shows the rejection of prices at key levels.

Image 4.20 – *Example of a bearish pin bar pattern (PAYPAL Holdings)*

Image 4.20 shows an example of a bearish pin bar at the resistance trend line. It indicates the explicit rejection of the price to trade above the resistance trend line. After this point, the price didn't show any signs of recovery and displayed a significant fall.

How To Use These Candlestick Patterns

Traders should not use these candlestick patterns independently to take trades. These patterns should only be used at predetermined key price levels (either support or resistance).

Besides, don't take a trade before the completion of the pattern. For example, if you are using a 1-hour timeframe, and after 30-45 minutes it looks like any of the aforementioned candlestick patterns, don't opt for the trade immediately, because the pattern might be negated or change in the remaining time. It's always better to plan a trade after the completion of the candlestick pattern.

It's always better to finalize a trading system and then apply these candlestick patterns. Otherwise, a trader loses control of their trading and ends up with many losing trades every day.

5

Price Action Trading Strategies

Do you know why racing horses' eyes are covered with blinkers or blinders? Those blinders are made of leather or plastic and are placed on both sides of the horse.

They reduce the angle of the horses' vision by over 75%, but still, all riders (especially in races) use them. Are they crazy?

Image courtesy Mohamed Noval (Unsplash)

The reason is pretty simple and straightforward.

Horses have eyes on the sides of their face, which means they have peripheral vision. This can easily provoke the horse to run in any direction unless they are made to remain focused.

When the riders attach the blinders, they cover the sides of the horses' visions and allow them to focus ahead. With the device's help, racing horses can concentrate better on the target, and they can run with astonishing speed.

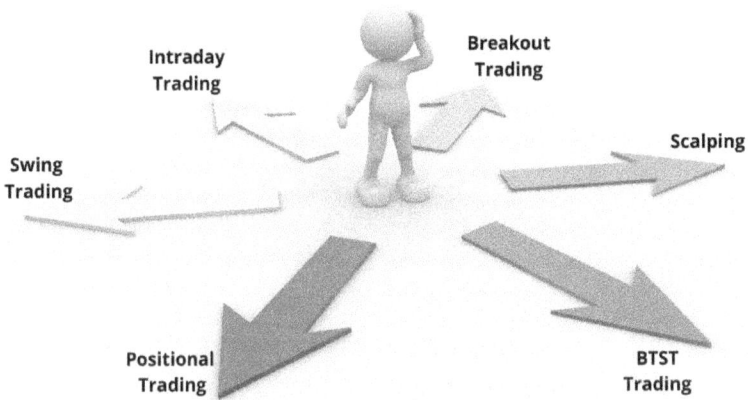

The same logic applies to all traders.

We have many trading types, such as swing trading, positional trading, and trend following.

If I stop at this point, traders will take trades in all possible trading styles and lose money. So, I will cover a few critical trading styles here, and you can pick any one trading style which suits your personality.

Please note that there is no need to implement all of them in your trading.

Swing Trading

Swing trading is a trading technique that seeks to capture a full swing when the price goes to a complete sideways zone.

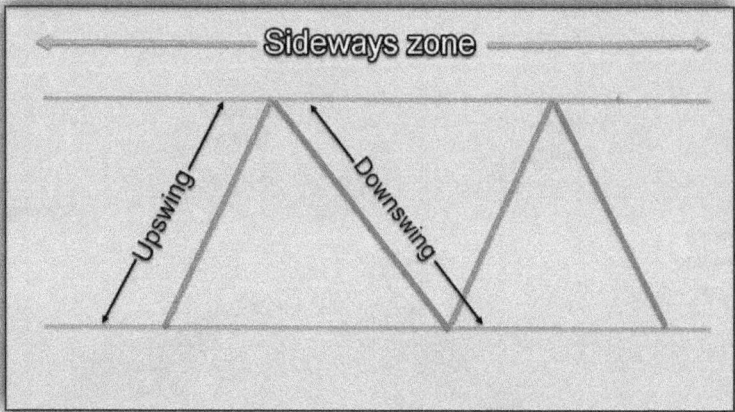

Image 5.1 – *Swing trading*

The idea is to get out of the trade before the opposing pressure comes in.

It means you look to book your profits before the market reverses.

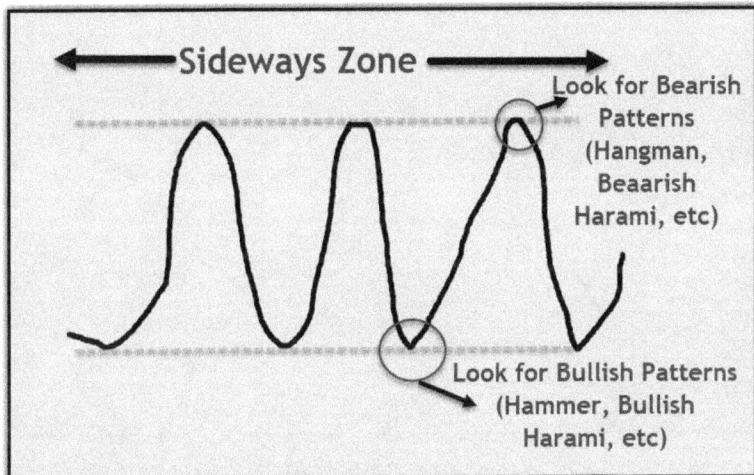

Image 5.2 – *Swing trading strategy*

Identify a range-bound stock or index as the first step.

For a long trade, look for bullish candlestick patterns such as bullish engulfing, bullish Harami, hammer, or morning star.

If you see the price confirmation, opt for a long trade above the chart pattern's high, keeping a stop-loss below the low of the chart pattern.

You can aim for the next resistance line as your target. Plan the trade only if the risk-reward ratio is greater than 1:2.

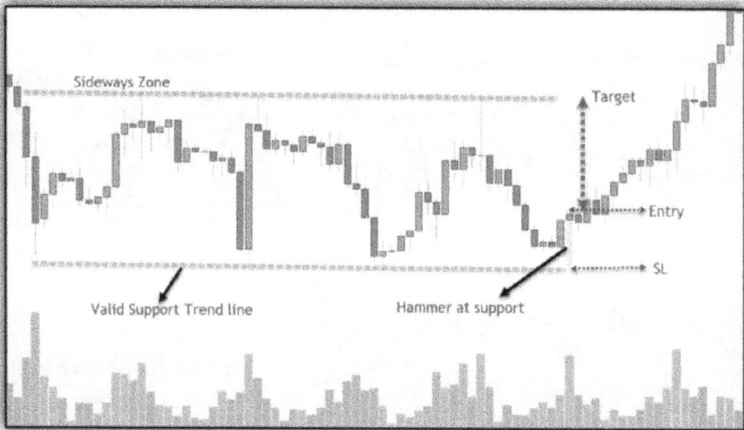

Image 5.3 – *Example of swing trading (long trade)*

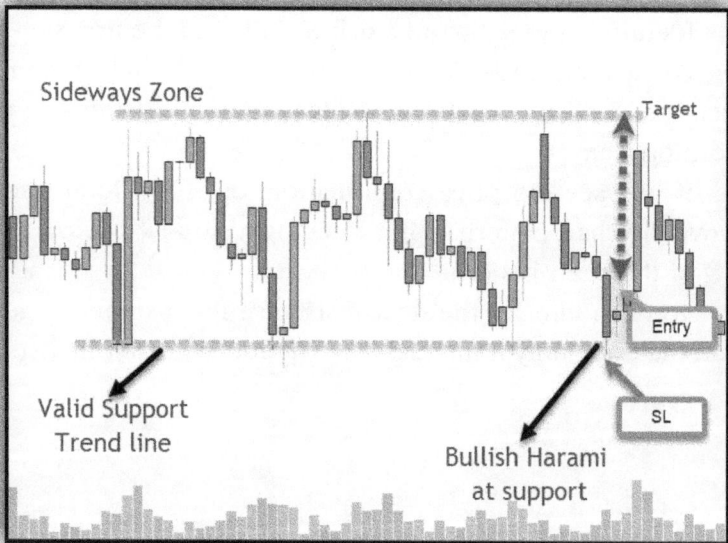

Image 5.4 – *Example of swing trading (long trade)*

Images 5.3 and 5.4 are examples of long trades in swing trading using candlestick patterns. In both cases, the price is in a sideways trend.

There were good support trend lines, and the prices displayed candlestick confirmation (hammer in Image 5.3 and bullish Harami in Image 5.4).

Hence, a long trade can be planned above the high of the confirmation candle, keeping a stop-loss below the confirmation candle's low.

The target will be the next resistance zone, as highlighted in the image.

For a short trade, look for bearish candlestick patterns such as bearish engulfing, bearish Harami, hanging man, evening star, and pin bar.

If you see the price confirmation, opt for a short trade below the chart pattern's low, keeping a stop-loss above the high of the chart pattern.

You can aim for the next support line as your target. Plan the trade only if the risk-reward ratio is greater than 1:2.

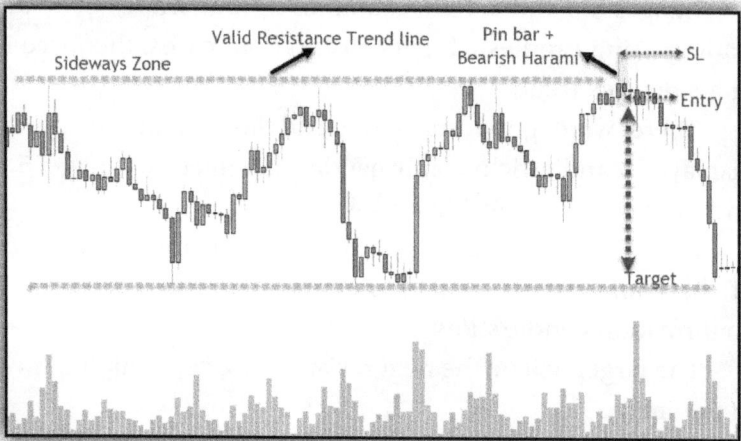

Image 5.5 – *Example of swing trading (short trade)*

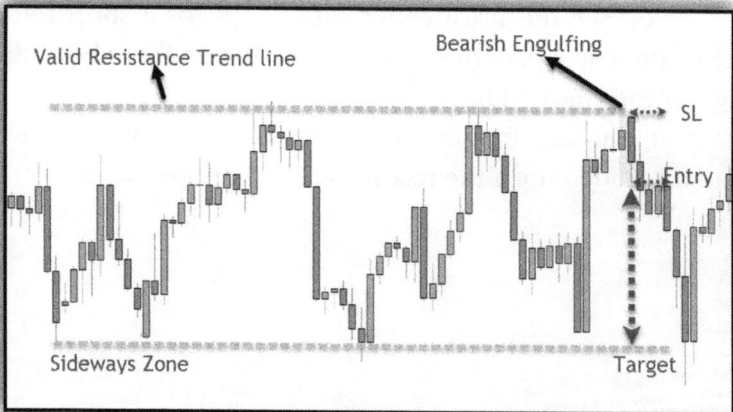

Image 5.6 – *Example of swing trading (short trade)*

Images 5.5 and 5.6 are examples of short trades in swing trading using candlestick patterns.

In both cases, the price is in a sideways trend. There

were good resistance trend lines, and the prices displayed candlestick confirmation (pin bar + bearish harami in Image 5.5 and bearish engulfing in Image 5.6).

Hence, a short trade can be planned below the low of the confirmation candle, keeping a stop-loss above the confirmation candle's high.

The target will be the next support zone, as highlighted in the images.

Trend Following

In this system, the trend plays a crucial role as all the trades will come in the direction of the trend.

For long trades, the prior trend should be on the upside. If the price shows healthy correction and a candlestick pattern, one can plan a long trade.

For short trades, the prior trend should be down. If the price shows a bounce and a candlestick pattern, one can plan a short trade.

Rules for Long Trades:

1. The price should be in a clear uptrend.

2. Healthy pullback.

3. The price should display a bullish candlestick pattern at the support line.

4. The risk-reward ratio should be a minimum of 1:1.5.

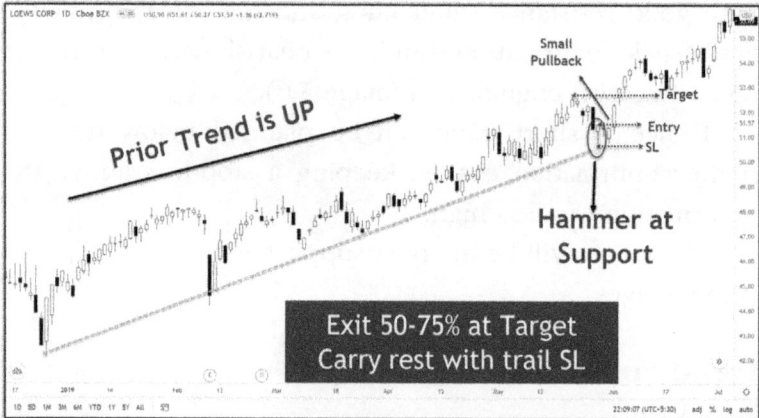

Image 5.7 – *Trend following a long trade (Loews Corp)*

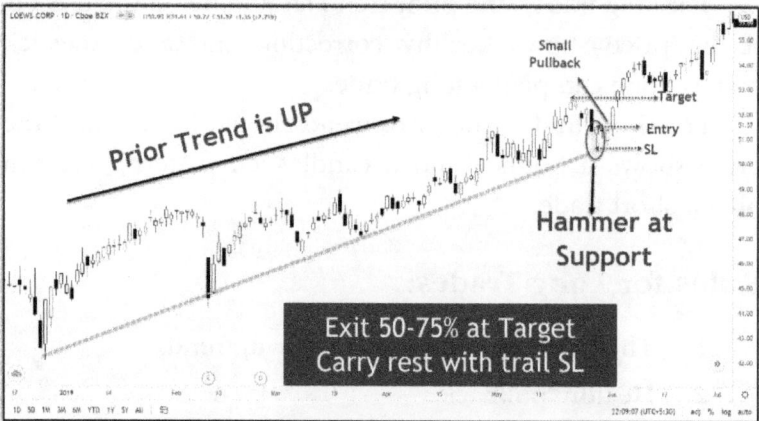

Image 5.8 – *Trend following a long trade (USD-CAD)*

Images 5.7 and 5.8 are simple examples of long trades using the trend following technique.

In both the cases, the prior trend is up, there was a healthy pullback, and candlestick confirmation occurred exactly at the support trend line (hammer in Image 5.7 and bullish engulfing in Image 5.8).

A trader can plan a long trade above the high of the confirmation candle, keeping a stop-loss below the low of the confirmation candle.

The previous swing high is the safe target (as the primary trend is up). Hence, we can plan to exit 50-75% of the position at the target and carry the remaining position by trailing stop-loss below every swing low.

Trailing stop-loss is the most critical aspect of the trend following system, as you never know where the trend will stop. In fact, it is the core logic of this trading approach. Sometimes, profits in one trade (using trailing SL) can absorb the loss of many failed trades.

Rules for Short Trades:

1.   The price should be in a clear downtrend.
2.   Healthy bounce.
3.   The price should display a bearish candlestick pattern at the resistance line.
4.   The risk-reward ratio should be a minimum of 1:1.5.

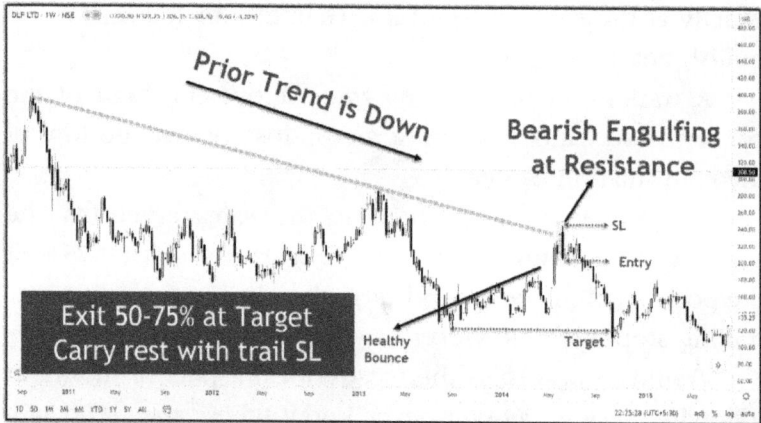

Image 5.9 – *Trend following a short trade (DLF)*

Image 5.10 – *Trend following a short trade (Ryder System)*

Images 5.9 and 5.10 are simple examples of short trades under the trend following technique.

In both cases, the prior trend is down, there was a healthy bounce, and candlestick confirmation occurred exactly at the resistance trend line (bearish engulfing in Image 5.9 and pin bar in Image 5.10).

A trader can plan a short trade below the low of the confirmation candle, keeping a stop-loss above the high of the confirmation candle.

The previous swing low is the safe target (as the primary trend is down). Hence, we can plan to exit 50-75% of the position at the target and carry the remaining position by trailing stop-loss above every swing high.

Swing trading and trend following are the two simple trading systems, and we can apply price action strategies directly in them.

If you are a beginner or an intermediate-level trader, mastering any one of these strategies is more than enough to taste success in trading.

The next chapter contains some advanced trading topics and a few trading systems based on those concepts. Again, feel free to skip it if you are a beginner and go directly to Chapter 7.

Breakout Trading

A breakout trading opportunity is nothing but a stock price moving outside a defined resistance level with increased volume.

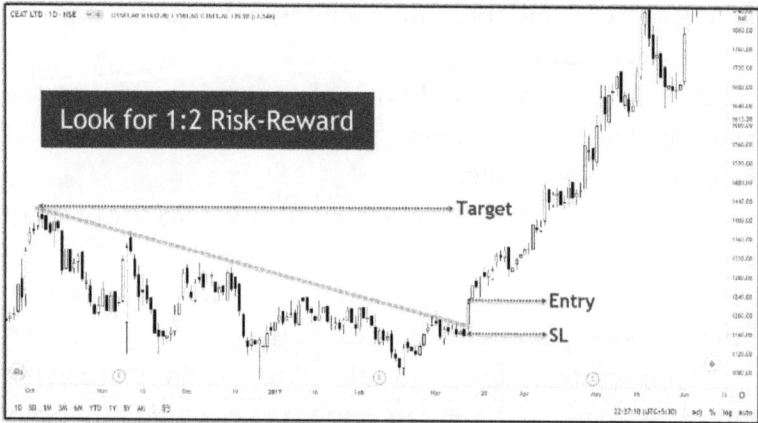

Image 5.11 – *Breakout trading system*

A breakout trader enters a long position after the price breaks above the resistance level, keeping a stop-loss below the resistance.

In this process, they either trail their stop-losses or target to exit at higher levels to make profits.

I have written a detailed book on this topic called *How To Make Money With Breakout Trading*. Please read this book to learn more about breakout trading.

6

Price Acceptance and Price Rejection

The fate of your trades is irrespective of your reputation, experience, and educational qualifications. They depend on only two things: entry and exit.

Everything else doesn't matter, and the market doesn't care about any other aspect except your entry and exit. Hence, it is necessary to have a deep understanding of the price to get success.

Price Rejection

Image 6.1 – *Support trading plan (A)*

Image 6.1 shows a support box in the USD-INR chart. The price has reached the support box.

If the smart money (the big people who already invested) still has a bullish view, what do they do? They pitch in and buy in large quantities.

Otherwise (if they are not bullish), buying will not come. Right?

Let's see what happened in the next candle.

Image 6.2 – *Support Trading Plan (B)*

Now carefully observe what happened the next day.

The price broke the lower levels of the support box. If the smart money is bullish (or keen to accumulate this), it is a wonderful opportunity for them. Hence, they entered with a large quantity, and their size was displayed as the rejection of the break of the support. This is called price rejection.

Once the price shows clear rejection from the smart money, there is a higher probability of the support box acting as support.

Hence, traders can plan a long trade above the rejection candle (or at the upper line of the support box, if you are looking for a safer trade), keeping a stop-loss below the rejection candle.

Image 6.3 shows the result.

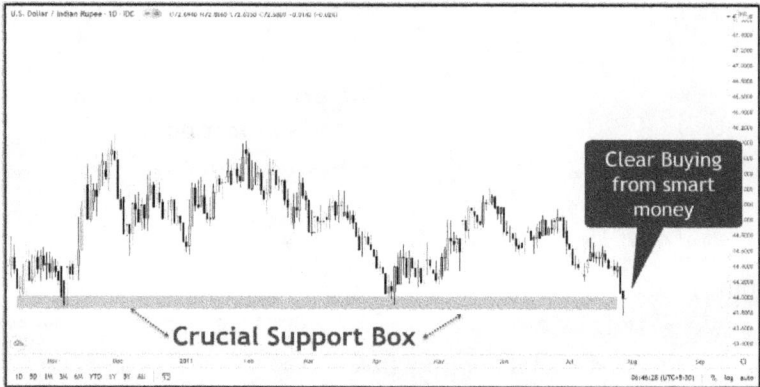

Image 6.3 – *Support trading plan (result)*

Price Acceptance

Image 6.4 – *Resistance trading plan (A)*

Image 6.4 shows a CEAT LTD daily chart.

There is a clear resistance trend line, and it looks like the price is taking resistance at the moment.

But if you observe carefully, you can identify two things (this is the beauty of price action trading):

1. The rejection candle is not strong.

2. Strong buying was witnessed in all the previous swings.

If the sellers are powerful, they have to take the price below the strong buying level. Right?

Image 6.5 – *Resistance trading plan (B)*

Image 6.5 shows what happened over the next few days. Sellers were clearly struggling to push the price downside.

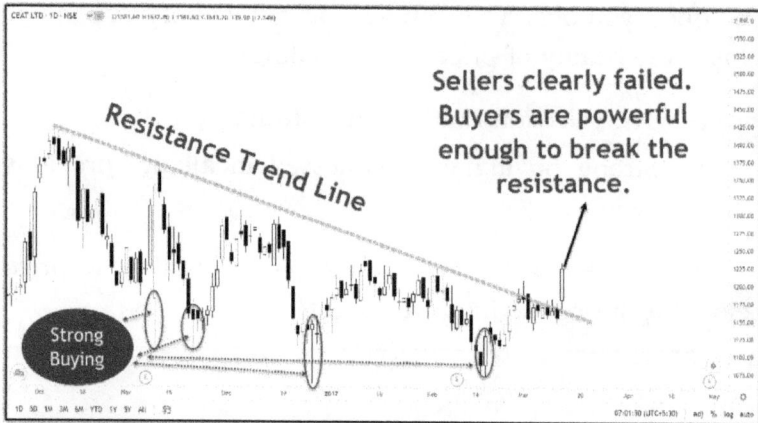

Image 6.6 – *Resistance trading plan (C)*

In Image 6.6, the failure of the sellers is clearly visible. Besides, buyers' dominance pushed the price above the resistance trend line and witnessed a strong close. This is called price acceptance.

Do you still think it is a good idea to think the resistance line acts as resistance?

I hope your answer is "no"!

We can then plan a long trade above the high of the accepted candle, keeping a stop-loss below the accepted candle. This has every probability of success, doesn't it?

You can see the result in Image 6.7!

Image 6.7 – *Resistance trading plan (result)*

Case Study 1: USD-INR

Image 6.8 – *Case study 1 (PA-1)*

Image 6.8 shows a USD-INR daily chart. There is a good resistance trend line and the price traded below the trend line for over a month.

But sellers' power is not enough to push the price to the downside (as it failed to make lower lows), and strong buying can also be witnessed at every swing low (highlighted as A in the image).

Besides, the price is trying to trade above the resistance trend line. It is a beautiful opportunity for sellers (if they are keen) to load their short positions. But their activity is so small that it created only two small pin bars.

This indicates a higher probability of price trading above the resistance trend line (which means the resistance line will not hold). However, we should not plan a long trade at this point. We need to wait for the entry of bulls (or the complete negation of sellers).

Image 6.9 – *Case study 1 (PA-2)*

Image 6.9 shows the same chart after one day of trading activity.

It is evident that sellers failed to push the price downside. Besides, buyers also entered and negated all the selling (highlighted as C).

This also supports our previous assumption. Hence, it is better to plan a long trade above the green candle's high, keeping a stop-loss below the low of the green candle. This trade has a high probability of success.

Image 6.10 – *Case study 1 (result)*

As I said earlier, only entry and exit decide the fate of your trade.

At the moment, I am focusing on entry. I will also provide a detailed explanation of exiting in the subsequent case studies.

Every trader can follow a straightforward exit strategy to book profits for 50% of the position at a 1:2 risk-reward ratio and carry the rest with the trailing SL concept (below swing low for long trades and above the swing high for short trades).

Case Study 2: Platinum Futures

Image 6.11 – *Case study 2 (PA-1)*

Image 6.11 shows a daily chart of Platinum Futures.

It has a good support trend line.

The price is near the support line, and the question is whether it will hold or not.

If you observe, the price failed to make higher highs, and the selling is strong at the swing highs.

We should not short at this moment as the scrip witnessed some buying (due to the small buying wick). We can plan a short trade once the price negates the selling.

Image 6.12 – *Case study 2 (PA-2)*

Image 6.12 provides the same chart, but after a few days of trading activity.

It is evident that buyers struggled to push the price to the upside (consolidation). Besides, there is a significant bearish candle (bearish engulfing) at the end: the last nail in the bulls' coffin.

This indicates price acceptance.

It means there is a higher probability of price going downside. Right?

So, we can plan a short trade below the low of the big bearish candle (or below the trend line for a safe trade), keeping a stop-loss above the high of the bearish candle.

Image 6.13 – *Case study 2 (result)*

Image 6.13 shows the result of this trade, and it conveys everything.

In this case, there are no good reference points to manage the exit. Hence, a trader can exit 50% for a 1:2 risk-reward ratio and carry the rest with the trailing SL concept.

Case Study 3: TCS

Image 6.14 – *Case study 3 (PA-1)*

Image 6.14 is a daily chart of TCS.

The price is moving in a clear sideways channel. In the end, buyers tried to push the price to the upside, but they failed miserably due to the sudden entry of sellers above the resistance zone.

In this candle, approx. 50% of the daily range is a selling wick. It indicates that buyers lack the firepower to fight with the sellers. Instead of taking a short trade, we can wait for one more candle to see who is more powerful.

Image 6.15 – *Case study 3 (PA-2)*

If you look at Image 6.15, the next candle is dominated by sellers. There was an open-high, and then the fall sustained for the entire day. Besides, the price failed to trade above the resistance line and high of the previous candle.

It confirms the presence of a robust selling force. Hence, we can plan a short trade below the low of the selling candle, keeping a stop-loss above the selling wick or the resistance trend line. We can aim for the support trend line as our target.

Image 6.16 – *Case study 3 (result)*

Image 6.16 shows the result of the trade. The price has reached our target of the support trend line.

I suggest exiting the trade at this moment. Can you think of the reason?

The answer is simple. There is a rejection candle with a big buying wick at the support line. So, instead of taking a risk, it is better to book the profit.

I am not saying it will go entirely upside from here, but there is a possibility of a slight bounce after seeing the rejection candle, and we are not sure to what level it will bounce. Hence, it is better to exit the trade.

If you are a risky trader, you can exit 50-75% of the position at the support line and carry the remaining position with the entry price as your stop-loss. In this way, even if the price hits your stop-loss for the small position, you end up making money for the large quantity.

Case Study 4: Nifty 15-Min Chart

The same price action concepts work very well, even in intraday or shorter time frames. But traders forget or ignore one crucial aspect when it comes to intraday trading or short-term trading.

Whenever we get into a lower timeframe, opportunities increase, but so does the risk and noise. So our money management rules should be designed to prevent erosion of our capital even if we get a few successive failed trades.

Image 6.17 – *Case study 4 (PA-1)*

Image 6.17 shows a Nifty 15-min chart. The below points are very clear from the chart:

- Buyers are struggling to push the price upside.
- Sellers are dominant (big red candles) in the channel.
- Buyers failed to push the price above the resistance trend line.

- Price showed acceptance close to the support trend line.

All these points indicate that there is a higher probability of the price breaking the support trend line.

We can either plan a short trade below the last red candle or wait for completion of one more candle (please note that in intraday trading, we may miss good opportunities due to waiting).

Image 6.18 – *Case study 4 (PA-2)*

Image 6.18 shows the same chart after the completion of another 15-min candle.

It is clear that sellers are in complete control. If you have already taken the trade, you are already in profit. If not, you can plan a short trade below the low of the last red candle, keeping a stop-loss above the high of the red candle (or above the support line). We can aim for the previous swing low (13,455) as our target.

Image 6.19 – *Case study 4 (Result)*

Image 6.19 shows the result of the trade, and it doesn't need any explanation!

Case Study 5: Bank Nifty 5-Min chart

Image 6.20 – *Case study 5 (PA-1)*

Image 6.20 presents an interesting scenario with a 5-min chart of Bank Nifty.

Bank Nifty showed a gap down open from the previous day's low. However, it failed to extend on the downside. It started to make successively higher lows.

However, strong selling can be witnessed in the three candles with large upper wicks below the resistance trend line, as shown in the image. At this moment, it is an equal fight between buyers and sellers.

All the sellers have kept their stop-loss above the day's high. Similarly, all the buyers have kept their stop-loss below the day's low.

Image 6.21 – *Case Study 5 (PA-2)*

Image 6.21 shows the same chart, but after the completion of 3 candles.

These three candles displayed acceptance of the price at the resistance trend line. The last candle also traded above the day's high, which means all the sellers should run to cover their positions.

It also indicates a trend day possibility with an upside range extension. (Both trend day and range extension are Market Profile concepts. Market Profile is highly beneficial for intraday traders and short-term traders. To know more about Market Profile, visit *www.profiletraders.in*.)

Hence, a trader can plan a long trade above the breakout candle's high, keeping a stop-loss below the breakout candle's low. One should apply the same logic of price action at every resistance level to manage the exit for their trades.

Image 6.22 – *Case study 5 (result)*

Image 6.22 shows the result of the trade. It witnessed a significant and quick move on the upside. The primary reason is that sellers ran for cover and indirectly became buyers (their stop-loss order is a buy order), and their eagerness to close the trade resulted in a massive move on the upside.

I hope all these explanations and case studies about price action are helpful. Did you notice I have not mentioned anything about volume yet? I did this intentionally for two reasons:

1. To focus your attention on the considerable information available from the price alone.

2. Many traders have read about the traditional usage of volume, and their minds would try to apply all those things if I had included volume.

The next chapter is dedicated entirely to volume, and you will find a completely different application of volume within.

7

What If I Told You Most Traders Use Volume the Wrong Way?

In price action trading, only two things are important: price and volume.

Until the previous chapter, we studied only price. In this chapter, we will explore volume.

I did not use the above title to catch your eye, but I have kept it because it is a fact.

This chapter has two modules: Volume Analysis Basics and Advanced Volume Analysis.

I am sharing the basic aspects of volume analysis in the beginning because advanced volume analysis will raise many questions in your mind, and it will shake the ideas or foundation of volume principles.

So, beginners and intermediate-level traders alike will benefit from the basic information about volume. More experienced traders will benefit more from the advanced concepts.

Volume Analysis Basics

Volume is nothing but the total number of buyers and sellers exchanging shares over a particular period.

For example, if the volume of XYZ stock on one trading day is 1 million, it means a group of people sold 1 million XYZ shares and another group of people have bought 1 million shares on the same day.

Traders should use volume as a confirmation tool and should never use it independently to initiate a trade (ignoring the price).

Price	Volume	Direction
Increase in Price	Increase in Volume	Bullish (It can go up)
Increase in Price	Decrease in Volume	Not Bullish
Decrease in Price	Increase in Volume	Bearish (It can go down)
Decrease in Price	Decrease in Volume	Not Bearish

The above table explains the price-volume relationship.

When the price is increasing along with an increase in volume, it is bullish in nature. But when the price is increasing with a decrease in volume, it is not bullish in nature. That does not mean we should look to short it because volume can go up again after the consolidation.

When the price is falling along with an increase in volume, it is bearish in nature. But when the price is falling with a decrease in volume, it is not bearish in nature.

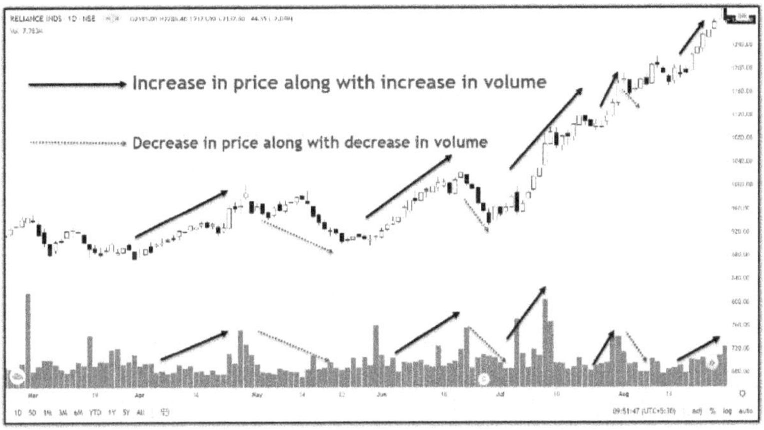

Image 7.1 – *Increase in price and volume*

Image 7.1 shows the case where both price and volume are increasing simultaneously. Whenever we see this kind of scenario, there is a higher probability of the price going upside.

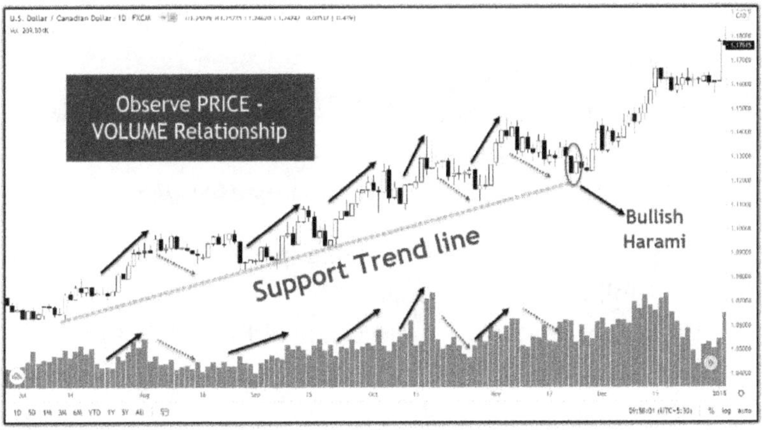

Image 7.2 – *Volume confirmation for a long trade (USD-CAD)*

Image 7.2 shows an example of a long trade in the trend following technique.

The prior trend is upside, there is a healthy pullback, and also, the price has shown a bullish Harami pattern at the support trend line. So from the price perspective, it looks good to take a long trade.

Now observe the volume. Every increase in price also witnessed an increase in the volume, and every decrease in price, followed by a decrease in volume. Hence, it looks good for the long trade.

Image 7.3 – *Volume confirmation is missing (USD-JPY)*

Image 7.3 shows a similar example for a long trade in the trend following technique.

The prior trend is up, there is a healthy pullback, and the price has displayed a bullish Harami pattern at the support trend line.

However, if you look at the price-volume relationship, it

tells another story. It has witnessed a volume spike during the downswings and has not seen a surge in volume in upswings.

It indicates the presence of serious sellers. Hence, it is not good to opt for a long trade even though the price has shown a bullish Harami pattern at the support trend line.

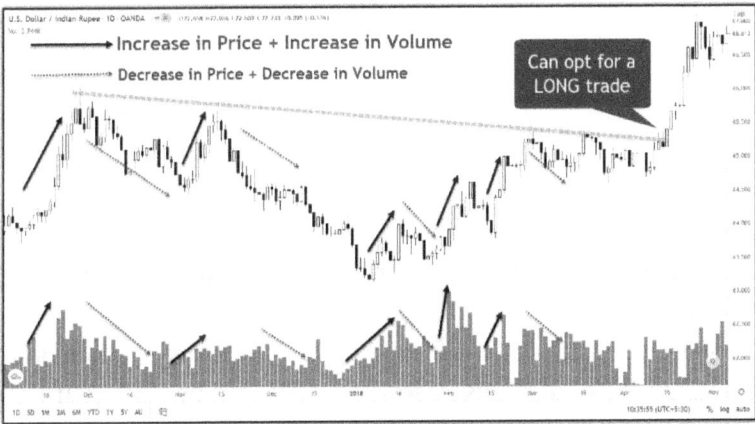

Image 7.4 – *Volume confirmation for a breakout trade (USD-INR)*

Image 7.4 shows an example of a breakout trade in USD-INR.

Look at the price-volume relationship carefully. Every price rise has witnessed increased volume, and every correction in price has caught less volume. This criteria is good for bulls and acts as confirmation from the volume side to opt for a long trade.

Image 7.5 – *Volume confirmation for a short trade (TATA Motors)*

Image 7.5 shows an example of a short trade in Tata Motors.

The prior trend is down, there is a healthy bounce, and the price also displays a few bearish candlestick patterns such as a bearish Harami and pin bar at the resistance trend line.

Now carefully look at the price-volume relationship. Every fall in price has witnessed an increase in volume, and every price rise has shown less volume. Hence, the volume indicates the strong presence of bears. Therefore, it is a good idea to opt for a short trade.

Advanced Volume Analysis

I want to give a small warning before I proceed with this part. If you are a beginner, please skip this part and go directly to the next chapter. You can use the concepts from Volume

Analysis Basics, and you can read this part after getting some experience.

The traditional idea or understanding of the price-volume relationship doesn't work all the time, and it misses many important aspects.

For example, traders say the price will go up only with increase in volume. In my opinion, this idea is not correct. The price can go up further with more volume, it can go up with medium volume, and it can also go up with less volume.

Do you think my idea is rubbish? Let's look at some charts.

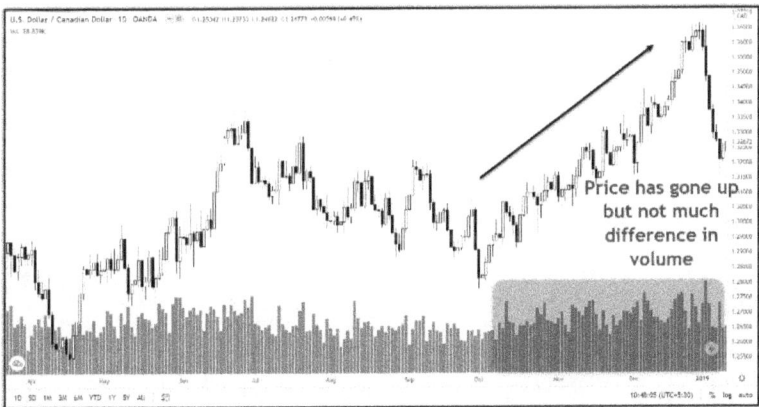

Image 7.6 – *Price-volume relationship (USD-CAD)*

In Image 7.6, the price has gone up from October to the end of December. But where is the increase in volume? The volume is almost the same compared to the average volume, isn't it?

Do you have a tough time digesting this fact? Let's look at Image 7.7.

Image 7.7 – *Price-volume relationship (USD-INR)*

Image 7.7 is a USD-INR chart in which the price has gone up from 64.25 to 68.75. But look at the volume part; it's less than the average volume, isn't it?

It clearly shows that the price can go up even with less volume.

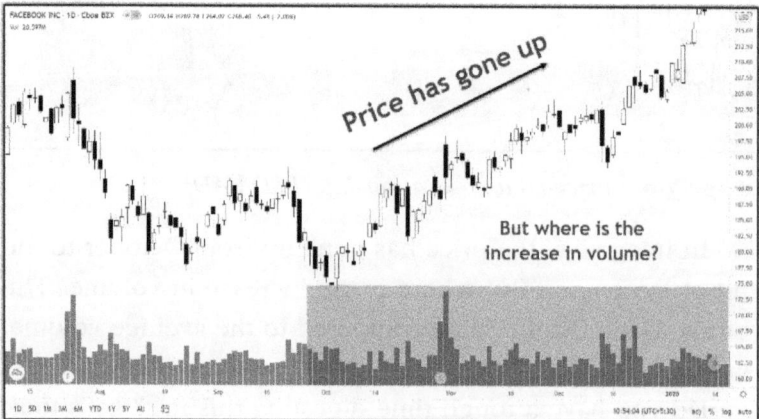

Image 7.8 – *Price-volume relationship (Facebook)*

Image 7.8 shows one more example in which the price has gone up without an increase in volume.

By now, at least, do you agree that the price can go up with more volume, medium volume, or less volume?

If you still have a tough time accepting and digesting this fact, please visit some charts and observe the volume part in the upswings of the price.

Image 7.9 – *Price-volume relationship (LIC)*

Now a simple chart to test your understanding.

Observe Image 7.9. A resistance trend line, and the price opened and closed above the trend line with a significant volume spike.

What is your view on this chart? Bullish? Bearish? Or no clarity?

If your answer is "bullish", then there is a serious mismatch between your understanding and reality. Let me explain in detail.

Do you agree that the resistance zone belongs to sellers?

Besides, sellers should be absent at the resistance zone

to give a further move on the upside.

But look at the breakout candle carefully. It has a selling wick that is about 50% of the body. It means 50% of them are sellers.

You developed a bullish view after looking at the big green volume spike, right?

But this volume spike indicates that 50% are sellers. This is where the analysis of many traders goes wrong.

Let's study one more example.

Image 7.10 – *Price-volume relationship (Tata Motors)*

Look at Image 7.10 carefully. What is your view on volume spikes A and B?

The price candle corresponding to volume spike A contains a buying wick of 40%, hence there are 40% buyers in the spike.

The price candle corresponding to volume spike B contains a buying wick of over 60%, hence there are 60%

buyers in the spike.

After clearing this major misconception, I can explain how I analyze the price-volume relationship.

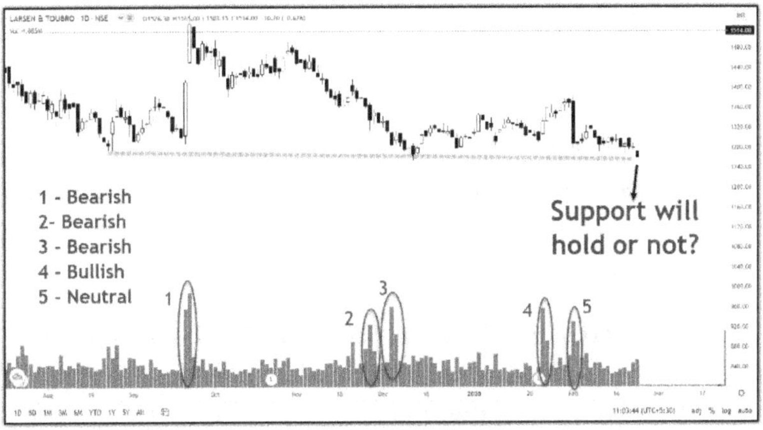

Image 7.11 – *Advanced price-volume analysis*

Earlier, we have learnt to use price to decide whether the support or resistance will hold or not. Now we will explore the same through volume, and later we can combine both price and volume to make a trading decision.

Image 7.11 shows a daily chart of LT, and now the price is near the support trend line. To decide whether the support will hold or not through volume, we need to analyze the significant volume spikes.

I have marked five significant volume spikes on the chart, and I analyzed these spikes as below:

- **Spike 1** – It looks bullish, but there is a selling wick and the price also fell later. Hence, I mark this spike as **bearish**.

- **Spike 2** – There is no buying wick and the price also fell later. Hence, I mark this spike as **bearish**.

- **Spike 3** – Again, there is no buying wick and the price also fell later. Hence, I mark this spike as **bearish**.

- **Spike 4** – Not much selling wick and the price has gone up later. Hence, I mark this spike as **bullish**.

- **Spike 5** – This spike is debatable. It has both buying and selling wicks, but the price fell after 2 days. Hence, I mark this spike as **neutral**.

Now there are 5 volume spikes in total. Among the 5, there are 3 bearish volume spikes, 1 bullish spike, and 1 neutral spike. Hence, there is a high probability of the price breaking the support trend line.

You can look at the result in Image 7.12.

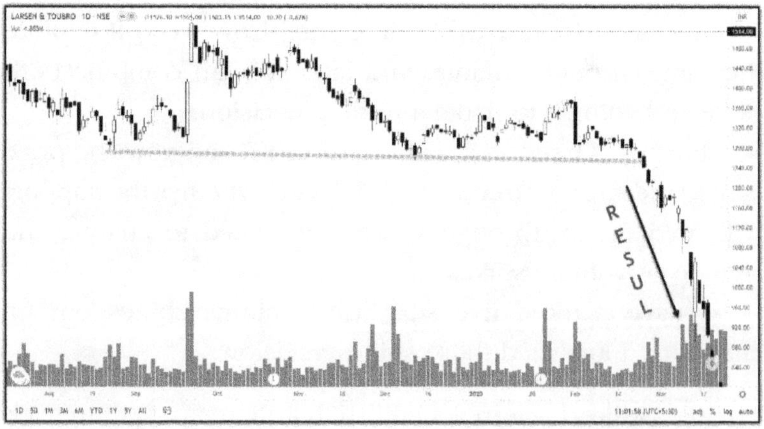

Image 7.12 – *Advanced price-volume analysis (result)*

I hope this information is useful.

If you want to know more about the price-volume relationship, please consider looking at the *Price Action Trading Strategy Guide* course (available at *online. profiletraders.in*).

8

The 4 Pillars of Successful Trading

Most traders give more importance only to technical analysis and ignore the remaining concepts. Please don't commit such a big blunder.

There are 4 pillars of successful trading:

1. Technical analysis
2. Money management
3. Psychology
4. Execution

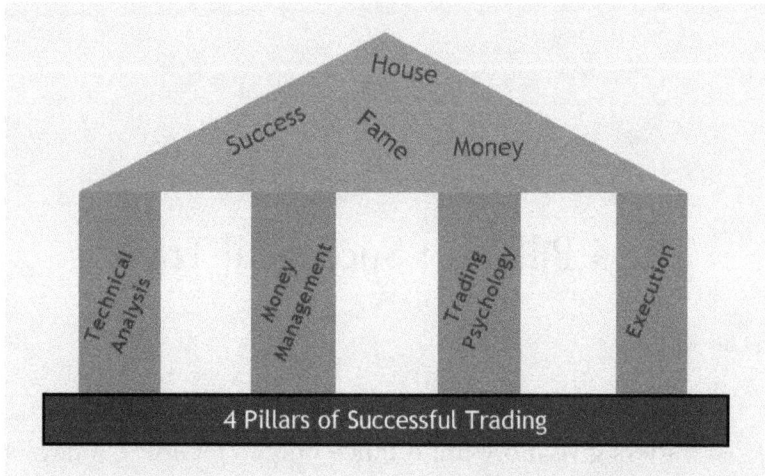

4 Pillars of Successful Trading

These concepts are similar to the 4 wheels of a car, and you will not be able to achieve trading success if you are missing even 1. Hence, give equal importance to all the concepts to achieve success in trading.

Pillar 1: Technical Analysis

In simple words, whatever you learned in the previous chapter is a small aspect of technical analysis.

Technical analysis is a method used to predict the future price movement of a stock/index by analyzing the old data in different ways. Technical traders believe current and past price action is the most reliable tool to predict future price movements. They don't use any fundamental information to make a trading decision.

Technical traders use price charts (the most popular one is the candlestick chart), indicators (there are thousands), and different representations of volume (volume profile, order flow) to analyze the price.

Pillar 2: Money Management

> *"Even a poor trading system could make money with good money management."*
> **– Jack D. Schwager**

Money management is a set of rules for allocating the required position size to reduce risk while aiming for good returns in trading.

There are many ways, but the right way always focuses on both reducing the losses and maximizing profits.

Before you pick any money management method, it is essential to ask yourself what type of trader you are, because one particular method suits positional traders and another suits intraday traders and scalpers.

I will explain both the techniques, but pick the method which suits your trading style.

For Positional Traders

For each trade, allocate 10% of your capital.

For example, if you have Rs. 1,00,000 as your capital, finalize script XYZ for trading, and (let's say) the CMP of XYZ is Rs. 100, then 10% of your capital is Rs. 10,000. So, you can buy 10,000/100 = 100 shares of XYZ.

Using this approach, your entire capital percentage risk per trade varies between 0.5%-2% (based on how deep your stop-loss is), which is adequate.

For Intraday Traders

Risk only 2% per trade on any trading day. Also, don't lose more than 5% on any trading day, which means you are not supposed to take more than 2-3 trades on any trading day.

Many traders suggest to risk only 1-2% of your capital even for positional trades, and they don't put an upper cap on the capital. This introduces some confusion while taking positional trades.

Let me explain with an example.

Assume your capital is Rs. 1,00,000.

You plan to risk 2% of your capital per positional trade, which is Rs. 2,000/trade.

You had shortlisted script XYZ – entry at 1000 and SL at 990.

Then the total number of shares to buy = Rs. 2,000/10 = 200 shares.

The capital required to buy 200 shares = 200 x Rs. 1,000 = Rs. 2,00,000.

But you don't have Rs. 2,00,000 capital in your account, do you?

So, the simple way is to deploy only 10% of your capital on one positional trade.

This will solve many problems for positional traders.

This problem may not arise if a trader is planning to take positional trades in futures, as leverage will take care of the additional capital requirement (but you need to take care of big gap opening risks).

Intraday traders also don't face this issue as most of them take trades in futures or options. In both cases, leverage is available, and it will look after the additional capital requirement.

To put it in simple terms:

- **Positional traders**: Deploy 10% of your capital per trade.
- **Intraday traders**: Risk only 2% of your capital per trade.

Pillar 3: Psychology

Psychology means the mental factors or emotions governing a situation or activity. So, when we say trading psychology, it implies the cognitive factors governing trading.

Four major emotions revolving around trading are greed, fear, regret, and hope. Please note that all these factors emerge because of a lack of knowledge.

Greed

Developing a compulsive attitude to generate more profits from every trade is greed. We lose money in some trades, we make small profits in a few trades, and only very few trades fetch big profits.

A trader can survive in markets without profits, but not without capital. Protecting capital is pivotal, and the next important aspect is consistent profit-making.

Friendly advice: Set process-oriented goals and not monetary goals. Think of protecting capital and surviving in the market for a more extended period.

Fear

Most of the fears in your mind are created from past bad experiences in trading. For example, say you are ready to take a breakout trade, but your mind hesitates to pull the trigger because in the past, you have lost money with some breakout trades and your subconscious mind associates the breakout trading concept with pain. Hence, there is hesitation in your mind.

In some cases, fear also occurs due to your upbringing. For example, if you have absorbed the thought that business is bad while growing up, then you face many difficulties in your trading.

The only way to get rid of fears in trading is by increasing your conviction in trading. You can do this by backtesting your system with more data, reading specific books on trading, or taking a particular trading course.

If you have any fears related to your upbringing, then identifying and acknowledging them is the most important step. Then you can use simple methods such as affirmations or practicing gratitude to get rid of these fears. If the issue persists, you can consult a mental coach or hypnotist.

Friendly advice: Plan your trade and trade your plan.

Regret

In trading, our regrets are never-ending. If you exit a trade and the price keeps moving in a favorable direction, you regret your exit decision. If you don't take profits from a trade and then the trade takes a turn into the negative zone, you regret your decision of not exiting.

Friendly advice:

1. Be satisfied with your decisions.
2. Keep learning and improving day by day, trade by trade.
3. Don't spend your energy regretting your choices if they are in line with your trading plan.

Hope

A trader starts hoping for some miracle to happen as soon as he deviates from his trading plan.

For example, a trader plans to buy a stock at 100 with 98 as the stop loss level and book profit at 104 level.

The price moves to 100, and he is in the trade.

After some time, the price moves to 104, but he didn't book the profit, as he starts hoping that short covering will come into the market soon and take his position to massive profit.

Now the market takes a U-turn. Our stock price moves back to 99, and now he starts to hope for a rebound. The price falls below 98, but he doesn't book the loss as he thinks a rebound is just around the corner. The price is now 96, and he is still living in the hope of a rebound.

What has happened in the above example is that he has lost control of his trading plan.

The pre-decided stop loss and the target are the 2 points where we need to act. Once we do not act on reaching those points, the situation is not in our control, and the decision we take after that is based on hope, which is a sign of weakness.

Friendly advice: Be ready with action points (stop loss and target) and act as per your trade plan. The market keeps throwing many good opportunities. Please don't allow any trade to be dependent on hope and then become hopeless.

Negative things affect the psychology of a trader. No matter how skilled a trader you are, you can't succeed in this business if you fill your mind with negative thoughts.

Below are some methods to get rid of negative thoughts from your mind:

Start positive: Start your day by reading a positive quote or book for some time, or by watching a positive or motivational video. When you think positive thoughts early in the morning, your mind carries these positive vibrations throughout the day. You will stay energetic and happy the entire day.

Gratitude: We always think about the objects or people that are not present in our life. This always creates unhappiness or incompleteness in our mind. It's good to think about the objects or people you desire; however, it's more critical to show gratitude for all the things or people you do have at the moment.

Every night before going to bed, think about all the things and people you have in your life now and feel happy about all these things. This behavior brings completeness and happiness in your mind, and it will increase your energy level to achieve further goals.

TV/phones: If possible, avoid watching TV or using phones before going to sleep. As per the latest studies, the bright light from TVs and phones stimulates the brain, affecting the secretion of melatonin, a hormone necessary for quality sleep. Lack of quality sleep will harm your mindset.

Avoid fights, gossiping, and arguments: Fights, gossiping, and arguments are significant sources of our negative thoughts. If you are angry, avoid conversations with people. It is better to take some time off to relax. Once you come out of your angry mood, compose your thoughts and then continue your discussion. Gossiping will not benefit anyone; use this time to read a good book or for any other good hobby.

Pillar 4: Execution

How One Idea Can Change Your Life

In 1931, Ted, a pharmacist, and his wife Dorothy, a former teacher, bought a small drug store in the town of Wall, South Dakota, US. They wanted to settle down in a small village that had both a school and a good church. Wall fulfilled these requirements, and hence they started their business in Wall by purchasing a tiny drug store.

Many tourists were traveling across the roads of Wall. However, no one was turning up at their medical shop. Summer season started, and the hopes of Ted and Dorothy began to go down. The main problem was how to attract tourists from the main road into the store.

Ted and Dorothy got an excellent idea. They started

serving cold water to anyone who walked into their store. They also put a few signboards on the main road with a route map to the Wall drug store and mentioned the free cold water.

With this idea, their business started growing, and today it has shops all over the world. Today, all branches of Wall drug store serve cold water to anyone who walks into their shops.

There is no need to look at their overall profits because they spend over $400,000 every year just on billboards!

What is your new idea to bring more discipline to trading? Remember, one idea can change your life!

Execution is the real Holy Grail in trading. Suppose you have an excellent positive expectancy system and clear money management rules. In that case, you can make money in trading in the long run if you execute the plan across all market conditions.

9

Trading for a Living

There is a vast difference between trading for fun and trading for a living.

Trading for fun is like a silly fight between siblings on a cozy bed in a bedroom.

Trading for a living is like a fierce fight involving you vs. Mike Tyson, Muhammad Ali, Rocky Marciano, and Manny Pacquiao simultaneously.

It is because trading was designed in such a manner. Anyone can enter and participate in the game. When you can take a trade, always remember you are fighting with many people who have spent decades in this business!

Never plan to take up trading for a living just because you have tasted some success in trading. The guidelines below are helpful if you are seriously considering taking up trading as a profession:

Guideline 1 – Passive Income

I learned so many things in my school and college days –

except for one thing, which is how to make money without putting in time and money. This is the art of passive income.

One has to plan a few passive income sources when they have a decent job.

Having a few passive income sources will increase your confidence. It will release the pressure to generate some money every month through trading to pay your monthly bills.

I am sure everyone has some talent or a passion for some activity. If you focus on and develop a little expertise in the subject, you can create a passive source of income.

I know everybody can't quit their job and become an entrepreneur, but most of us can begin something small today that can't be taken away.

I can give a few hints:

If you are good at photography, upload your good photos online. Many portals pay for good photos. For more information, check out:

- *submit.shutterstock.com*
- *freeimages.com*
- *pixabay.com*
- *gettyimages.in*
- *istockphoto.com*

If you are creative, you could try to design cover pages for ebooks. Do you know how ambitious Amazon is with its KDP project? Mark my words, you will see a hell of a lot of ebooks in the next few years, and all those ebook authors need attractive cover photos (by the way, the cover page of this book was also created in a similar way. That's his side hustle!).

Check out *fiverr.com* for more opportunities.

If you are good at video editing, help YouTubers out. Many successful people want to start their own YouTube channel, but they are biding their time as they don't know how to edit their videos.

If you are good at teaching something, create a course for *udemy.com* or *urbanpro.com*. If the content is good, then it will fetch you money, even when you are sleeping!

Suppose you are good at yoga and meditation. You can start teaching it online. The entire world is your target audience, as everyone is trying to improve their immunity due to COVID-19. Find one such inspiring success story here: *kushiyogalaya.com/onlineyogaclasses*.

Like me, you can also write a self-help book. If the content is useful and you do a little marketing, you could get some money every month. Check out *kdp.amazon.com* for more details.

Guideline 2: Zero Debts

If you have a monthly commitment (EMI) towards any loan, it would add extra pressure to your trading career as you would have to generate that amount every month.

Sometimes, there may be no opportunities in the market, or if you fail to make money in the market, extra pressure will be created in your mind, which impacts your trading decisions.

Hence, it is better to clear all your pending loans before thinking of taking up trading as a full-time business.

Guideline 3: Savings

You should save enough money to run your family for at least one year.

If you need Rs. 1,00,000 (approximately 2,000 USD) per month for all your expenses, then you'd have to save Rs. 12,00,000 (approximately 24,000 USD) before taking up trading as a full-time business.

This amount is excluded from your trading capital, which you require for your trading. In this case, your trading results will not impact your mindset, and you will also not face any emotional pressure from your family members.

Guideline 4: Trading Results

Trading looks very simple when a beginner makes some quick money. However, you should realize that market conditions are always dynamic and it requires enormous skills to make consistent money in the market.

So it is better to measure your trading success before you take the extreme step of becoming a full-time trader. It is a good idea to consider yourself a successful trader only when:

1. You've made at least six months of your current salary from trading profits in total, and

2. You've made profits for three consecutive months.

Guideline 5: Trading Capital

The above parameters alone are not sufficient to enable you to quit your current job and jump into trading. You should have adequate trading capital to make profits in the market.

If you can make 10% returns every month (10% per month is good returns as per any trading expert), you would need a minimum of Rs. 10,00,000 (approximately 20,000 USD) as your trading capital if your monthly expenses are around Rs. 1,00,000 (approximately 2,000 USD).

A Small Warning

One of the most significant advantages and disadvantages of full-time trading is that you are the boss and don't have to report to anybody. Usually, we are used to the 'reporting' style of work, and this freedom may work against you if you don't have serious trading plans and goals. You should keep the following points in mind when you become a full-time trader:

- You should not take breaks from trading days for any reason. Because opportunities may come at any moment, you should be ready to grab them on all trading days.

- Your laziness can cost you dearly in the market. Trading is your business, and you should be ready like a businessperson before the open of the market. You have to finish your exercise, meditation, bath, etc. before looking at the market open. If you cannot concentrate on the market at home, hire a single-seat desk in any office (nowadays, you can hire a single-seat desk for monthly rent including an internet connection, maintenance, coffee, etc.).

- All successful traders maintain a trading journal, and hence it is a good idea to log all your trades with entry, exit, SL price, etc. You should review these trades on a periodical basis and evaluate your trading skills.

- Usually, in all other professions, we have a supporting environment. However, in trading, it isn't easy to have such an environment. Hence, you should develop a circle of profitable traders and be involved in monthly gatherings or other meetings. If possible, attend major events on trading like Traders Carnival, seminars conducted by experts, etc.

10

How to Make Money Trading Without Quitting Your 9-to-5 Job

Ask any established trader what their most important tip for the people who are aiming at full-time trading is and every one of them will tell them to not quit their current job immediately.

If you have a 9-to-5 job, you can still earn some passive income from trading by following specific steps. These steps will help you improve your trading skills while working 9-to-5 and still allow you to enjoy your life.

But any person has to overcome the following roadblocks to get better results in trading:

- **Responsibility** – Trading is all about decision making (either buy or sell), and one has to take 100% responsibility for their decisions. Unlike in an office, you can't blame management or colleagues here.

- **One man battle** – Most of the time, you will be

alone in trading. The majority of the people lose money in the stock market, so if you try to stay in a group, there is a high probability of getting bad trade results. It's better to stay aside from the group and focus on your own trading.

- **Motivation** – You have to find your own inspiration in trading. You don't get any target reports or performance assessment reports in trading. Besides, there is no boss to monitor your work. The market is the supreme boss here, and it will reward everyone based on their merit.

Here are 8 steps and tips that will help you to make money in trading while working your 9-to-5 job:

Step 1: Pick the Right Trading System

It is essential to have the right trading system with a suitable timeframe that complements your personality and schedule.

For example, if you have a tight schedule at your 9-to-5 job, there is no point in looking for trade opportunities in a 5-minute chart. Because a 5-minute chart demands more screen time, with your work schedule, you will not be able to do justice to both your work and trading.

Opportunities do exist across all timeframes. Any intelligent person will pick a suitable timeframe, wait for the proper trade setup, and manage the trade within their money management limits.

The two essential trading methods suitable for working professionals are positional trading and intraday trading.

- **Positional trading**: It is a type of trading in which a trader carries the positions overnight for a few days or weeks. BTST trades, STBT trades, or any trading type with a holding period of a few days to a few weeks falls under positional trading.

- **Intraday trading**: It is a type of trading in which you have to close the trade on the same day. Many people believe that intraday trading demands 100% screen time, but that is not correct. If you have a trading system, this screen time can be reduced by over 75% using tools such as alert mechanisms, using SL-M trigger orders, or partial/full algo trading.

Tip 1: Check your work schedule and decide whether you want to become an intraday trader or a positional trader. If you pick intraday trading, please note you get more trade opportunities, and hence the noise and failure rate will also be higher.

Step 2: Select the Right Trading Instrument

We have 3 trading instruments in the stock market:

1. Equity
2. Futures
3. Options

So, a trader should know how these trading instruments work.

Let us take an example to understand better.

Assume one trading account has Rs. 3,30,000 (3.3 lakhs). ACC Current Market Price CMP is 1,620.

Assume ACC went up 5% (81 points) in the next 2 trading days (for explanation's sake).

Case 1: Equity

With 3.30 lakhs, one can buy 203 shares.

Profit made due to 5% upside movement is Rs. 16,443 (203 shares x 81 points).

ROI on Capital is 5%.

Case 2: Futures

With 3.30 lakhs, a trader can buy 1 lot (500 shares). One can verify future details using the following link: *zerodha.com/margin-calculator/span.*

Profit made due to 5% upside movement is Rs. 40,500 (500 QTY x 81).

ROI on capital is 12%.

Case 3: Options

With 3.30 lakhs, one can buy 7,500 QTY of 1,700 CE of ACC (assuming premium at 42).

Profit made due to 5% upside movement is Rs. 2,43,000 approx (IV at 40%).

ROI on capital is 74%.

ROI varies drastically across all 3 trading instruments.

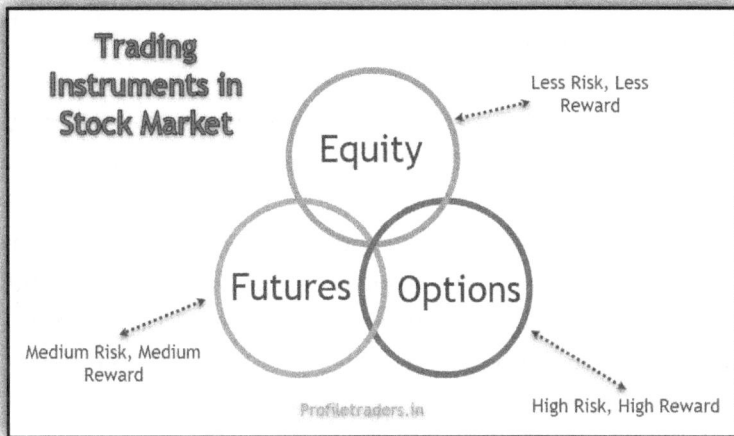

Trading Instruments in Stock Market

Equity — Less Risk, Less Reward

Futures — Medium Risk, Medium Reward

Options — High Risk, High Reward

Profiletraders.in

Please note this explanation is not intended to encourage trading in options. F&O trading carries the highest risk levels, and the above description gives an overview of how the three trading instruments work by offering various degrees of risk and reward.

Tip 2: Start your trading with equity. Even if you get failures, you lose less money. You should try futures only when you are already making profits with equity trading. Similarly, you should try options only when you are already making profits with futures trading. Please note these derivative products just amplify your trading results!

Step 3: Avoid System Hopping

Say a person starts to learn how to drive a car. Today he starts with one car and gets to know all the basics. Tomorrow, he will start the process again with another vehicle, and this process continues. Every day, he continues learning with a different car. Do you think he will be able to complete the learning process?

It is better if he sticks to one car until he completes the learning process and can then drive any car he wishes.

But when it comes to trading, many people forget this process. People study one indicator or trading concept and try it for some time. When they get some failures, they immediately start using another system or looking to add one more indicator to their trading system, thinking it will fix it. It's a vicious cycle!

"All you need is one pattern to make a living."
– Linda Raschke

One can finalize a trading system after complete backtesting. If the system shows positive expectancy in the long run, then it can be deployed in trading. But ensure you don't lose more than 2% of your capital on any trade.

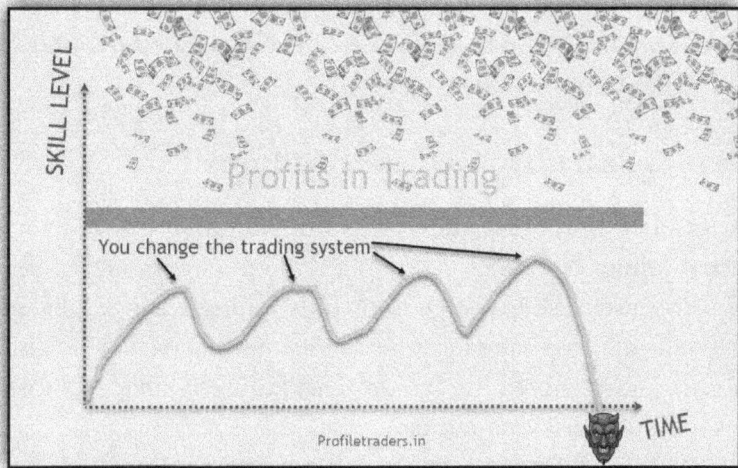

Tip 3: Take an oath not to change your trading system for one whole year. Study every mistake, identify the root cause behind the mistake, and avoid the mistake next time.

Step 4: Improve Trading Psychology

Psychology means the mental factors or emotions governing a situation or activity. So, when we say trading psychology, it implies cognitive factors governing trading.

The four primary emotions revolving around stock market trading are greed, fear, regret, and hope. Suppose a trader works to develop more conviction in his trading system and improves his psychology (to avoid unnecessary trades, ride profits, and adhere to money management rules). In that case, these issues get dissolved automatically.

Tip 4: Psychology plays a crucial role alongside the trading system. Affirmations, developing gratitude for what you have, and meditation all help to develop a better mindset and make better trading decisions.

Step 5: Learn To Face Your Failures

All of our upbringings taught us one common thing, which is that failure is bad.

No parent likes to see their kids failing their exams, so they take all possible measures to ensure they pass. This kind of upbringing stores the lesson that "failure is unacceptable" in their subconscious minds.

Because of this one reason, many traders feel bad (sometimes even pathetic) even if they lose a little money in a trade. It's not because they can't afford that money; it's because they have a tough time digesting the failure!

After that, they develop a vengeful attitude and take more trades or risk more per trade to get back the money from the market as soon as possible. Needless to say, they end up losing more money.

To become a successful trader, learn to digest failures, work on consistent improvements

Learn to digest the losses (keep it small)	Avoid mistakes, trust your system and work on psychology	Fine-tune the trading system, avoid looking at other traders' profit screen shots	Learn to ride your profits, keep ego in check, learn to compound the position and always believe market is supreme!
Lose Less	**Breakeven**	**Small Profits**	**More Profits**

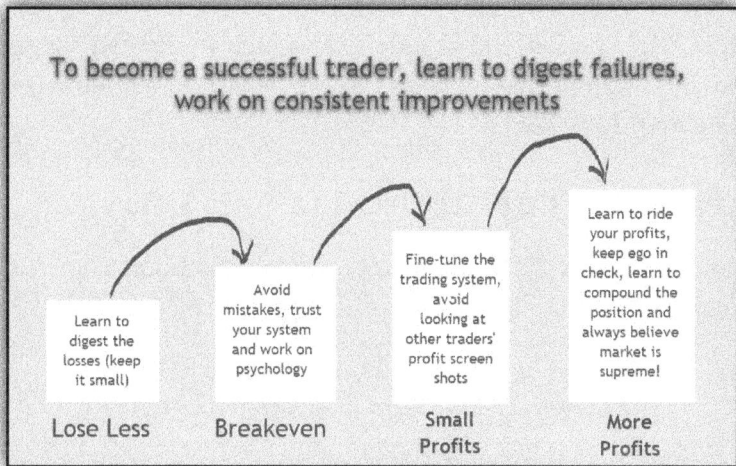

Tip 5: Failure is inevitable in trading. Nobody wins 100% of their trades. A successful trader loses less money when he is wrong and makes more money when he is right.

Step 6: Know the Difference Between 'a Good Trade' and 'Good Trading'

The difference between a good trade and good trading is a lot of money. Most traders feel high when they get more profits in one trade and hence always run behind one such big trade.

It is not wrong to get one good trade to make more profits, but a person will lose many small opportunities to make consistent profits if they run behind it. Besides, traders commit many mistakes such as taking more trades in a day, taking unnecessary trades, etc.

Tip 6: A trader can only control how much he will risk in a trade. The market will decide how much to reward for the trade. So follow the entry and exit mechanism as defined in your trading system.

Step 7: Don't Get Addicted to Your Salary

Nassim Nicholas Taleb, author of the famous book *The Black Swan*, once said:

> *"The three most harmful addictions are heroin, carbohydrates, and a monthly salary."*

Most people have some dreams in their heart, but they don't pursue their dream because they are addicted to their salary. Most of us start to make some commitments (house loan, car loan, etc.) whenever we get into a new position. We can't even survive if we don't get the salary for a month because of these commitments.

Profits from trading vary every month based on the market conditions. If you have some financial commitments every month, it always introduces some pressure even if you are a salaried person. Hence, it is better to stay out of these commitments when you are learning to trade.

When you don't have any commitments, you don't get addicted to your salary; your mind is free most of the time, which allows you to make better trading decisions.

Try to add 20-25% of your salary every month to another savings account. If you are already successful at trading, then you can add this amount to your trading capital. Otherwise, park the amount in some source where you get some returns and where it's also easy to withdraw from.

Tip 7: Don't invest in depreciating assets by taking a loan. Many people buy a house, taking over 75% of the value through a bank loan. When they get into challenging situations like the loss of a job or a health emergency, they suffer more as they will not be able to sell the house and can't pay the EMI. A simple way to avoid this problem is to reverse the calculations. Never buy a house until you save at least 50-75% of the cost through savings.

Step 8: Remember That Life Is More Precious Than Trading

Trading is important. Making money in life is also vital, but this life is always more precious than all of them. What is the point of having tons of money if you can't enjoy it? What is the benefit of becoming a successful person if you are not happy?

Tip 8: Every month, visit a new place. You don't have to plan an expensive vacation; nice nearby places like a forest or a beach are also fine. Develop a hobby to stay fit; it could be hitting the gym, practicing yoga every day, or playing some game.

Final Words

I genuinely hope that you have gained some useful knowledge about price action trading.

I also hope it will play a decisive role in your trading

career. I hope to create and spread a positive impact on the lives of others through this book.

Now that you have read my book, I ask that you please do one of two things (or both) if you have some time.

1. If you have enjoyed this book, PLEASE leave a kind review on Amazon. As an independent author, word of mouth is my only means of advertising. Amazon link: *amzn.to/2Zb86uO*

2. No book is perfect. If there are any errors, omissions, or anything you would like to see added, please email me at indrazith.s@gmail.com. I promise a quick, personal response.

I would LOVE to hear your success stories, comments, and suggestions!

Signing off,

Indrazith Shantharaj (www.profiletraders.in)

Price Action Trading Course

If you need more clarity on price action trading or want to see more examples of the price-volume relationship, then please take the online course below:

Register at **online.profiletraders.in**.

What's Included?

- 3-month access to the course (you can watch it any number of times)

- WhatsApp support
- Quizzes to test your knowledge

Intraday Trading Course

Intraday Trading *is the most debated and misunderstood topic in the trading community.*

Every day we hear many scams related to intraday trading, which promises huge returns.

Unfortunately, many beginners who believe in get-rich-quick schemes fall for them and lose their hard-earned money.

However, many successful intraday traders make their living just by doing intraday trading.

Let us say you get the opportunity to drive a Formula 1 car.

What would you say?

"The Formula 1 car does not work!", *or* **"I do not know how to drive a Formula 1 car."**

If you were sensible, you'd pick the second statement,

right?

The same explanation goes for intraday trading.

There is no point in debating whether intraday trading is profitable or not.

It is only a type of trading in which you have to close the trade on the same day.

If you are right, you make money; if you are wrong, you lose money.

If you want to learn intraday trading, try the **INTRADAY TRADING ONLINE COURSE.**

Go check it out now at: **online.profiletraders.in.**

What's Included?

- 3-month access to the course (you can watch it any number of times)
- WhatsApp support
- Quizzes to test your knowledge

Other titles by Indrazith Shantharaj,
published by Manjul Publishing House

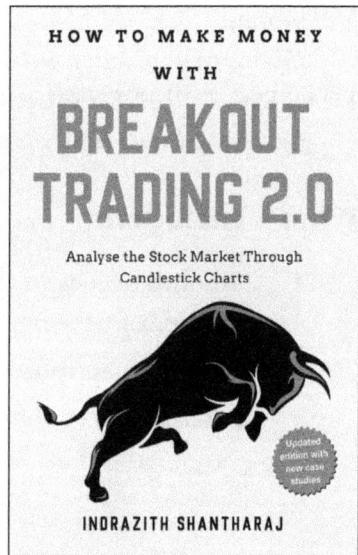

HOW TO MAKE MONEY WITH
BREAKOUT TRADING
Analyse the Stock Market Through Candlestick Charts
INDRAZITH SHANTHARAJ

HOW TO MAKE MONEY WITH
BREAKOUT TRADING 2.0
Analyse the Stock Market Through Candlestick Charts
Updated edition with new case studies
INDRAZITH SHANTHARAJ

www.ingramcontent.com/pod-product-compliance
Lightning Source LLC
Chambersburg PA
CBHW031941190326
41519CB00007B/613